Lan . .
LAKE GENEVA AND WESTERN
SWITZERLAND

a countryside guide

Reinhard Scholl

SUNFLOWER BOOKS

First edition © 2009
Sunflower Books™
PO Box 36160
London SW7 3WS, UK
www.sunflowerbooks.co.uk

ISBN 978-1-85691-356-0

Ibex near Gornergrat (Walk 29)

Important note to the reader

We have tried to ensure that the descriptions and maps in this book
are error-free at press date. The book will be updated, where
necessary, whenever future printings permit. It will be very helpful
for us to receive your comments (sent to the publisher's address above
or to mail@sunflowerbooks.co.uk).

  We also rely on those who use this book — especially walkers —
to take along a good supply of common sense when they explore.
Waymarking in Switzerland is excellent, but nature is dynamic: *storm
damage, landslides, floods or avalanches may make a route unsafe at
any time*. If the route is not as we outline it here, and your way ahead
is not secure, return to the point of departure. *Never attempt to
complete a tour or walk under hazardous conditions!* Please read
carefully the notes on pages 64-69 and the introductory comments
at the beginning of each tour and walk (regarding road conditions,
equipment, grade, distances and time, etc). Explore *safely*, while at
the same time respecting the beauty of the countryside.

*Cover photograph: children playing the alphorn on their Alpine meadow
   in the foothills of Mount Moléson, Fribourg Alps (Walk 14)*
Title page: reflections in Lac d'Arpitetta (Walk 27)

Photographs: the author
Maps: Sunflower Books, based on the 1:25,000 maps of the Swiss
   Federal Office of Topography (see page 67).
Sunflower Books and 'Landscapes' are Registered Trademarks.
A CIP catalogue record for this book is available from the British
   Library.
Printed and bound in China: WKT Company Ltd

❋ Contents

4   Landscapes of Lake Geneva and Western Switzerland

Winter walking in the Jura (Walk 10)

✿ Preface

If Switzerland didn't exist, you'd have a hard time dreaming it up: a small country with around 2700 municipalities bundled into 26 fiercely independent small self-governing regions — the cantons (the geographical boundaries of which can be puzzling at the best of times); four national languages (and that doesn't include English); a canton in which the lower valley speaks French and the upper valley German (where a street that begins as Route de la Gemmi ends as Gemmistrasse); a country with a strong democracy and where frequent voting is part of Swiss life; where the last armed conflict was a short civil war in 1847; one of the richest countries in the world and the site of multinational companies; known for banks, watches, cheese, chocolate, tourism; where 'Swissness' is associated with stability, fairness, direct democracy, punctuality, and quality.

And if that were not enough, it is a country blessed with a most dramatic and spectacular landscape. Mountains, glaciers, lakes, rivers, gorges, and waterfalls are plentiful natural elements into which cultural influences blend. Switzerland is a hiker's paradise (you would expect nothing less of a country which has an article in its constitution regulating the responsibilities of those who maintain the thousands of kilometres of hiking paths), and boasts the world's best public transport system, despite being arguably the most mountainous country in Europe. In Switzerland you may well find a mountain hut or comfortable hotel on top of a summit which is the terminus of a spectacular train or cable car ride, but there is still plenty of space where you will hardly meet a soul — perhaps only ibex.

This guide covers the western part of Switzerland, comprising:

• The region around **Lake Geneva** (Lac Léman in the local French), including the towns of Geneva, Lausanne and Montreux. Montreux and its lakeside is also known as the Swiss Riviera, a region where the Alpine meets the Mediterranean and where snow and palm trees are never far from each other.

• The **Swiss Jura** (partly French-, partly German-

5

SWITZERLAND IN A NUTSHELL: GEOGRAPHIC FACTS

Country: Die Schweiz (German), la Suisse (French), la Svizzera (Italian), la Svizra (Romansch) — in the four national languages. Confoederatio Helvetica (Latin), abbreviated CH: for internet websites, vehicle registration, and international postal services

Area: 41,293km^2/15,936mi^2 (about twice the size of Wales and half the size of South Carolina; about the same size as The Netherlands). If the topography of Switzerland is taken into account, ie, if the 'mountainous bumps' are flattened out, the surface area of Switzerland would be 12.5% bigger.

Distance: north to south 220km/137mi, east to west 348km/216mi

Borders: France to the west, Germany to the north, Austria and the principality of Liechtenstein to the east and Italy to the south

Largest cities: Zurich 350,000 (greater metropolitan area 1.1m); Geneva 179,000 (0.5m); Basel 163,000 (almost 0.5m); Berne 122,000 (capital; 340,000); Lausanne 118,000 (310,000)

Population: 7.6m, of whom about one-fifth are non-Swiss citizens

Population density: 184/km^2

Government: Parliamentary Federal State since 1848, direct democracy

Cantons: 20 full cantons, 6 half cantons; 2706 municipalities

Languages: Four national languages: German (64%), French (20%), Italian (7%), Romansch (1%), others (8%). About half the population speaks English.

Landscape: Three main types — the Alps, the hilly Swiss Mittelland from Lake Constance to Lake Geneva, and the Swiss Jura, a chain of low mountains separating Switzerland from France

Highest peaks: Dufourspitze (4,634m/15,203ft) in the Valais, on the border with Italy, is the highest — and the second-highest mountain in Western Europe after Mont Blanc (France); Dom (4,545m/14,911ft), also in the Valais, is the highest Swiss mountain entirely on Swiss soil. Around 23% of Switzerland is at an altitude higher than 2000m and 2% higher than 4000m; the average altitude is 1307m. Depending on how you count them, there are a few dozen peaks in Switzerland higher than 4000m, about two-thirds of which are in the Zermatt area.

speaking), a vast plain up to around 1600m with lush pastures and forests and which (this is the most beautiful theory) God created so that you can admire the chain of the Alps. It extends about 150km and stretches from near Lake Geneva almost to Basel, covering about 10 per cent of the country. Hikes up the four highest peaks of the Swiss Jura are included in this guide: Mont Tendre (1679m), La Dôle (1677m), Le Chasseron and Le Chasseral (both 1607m).

• The mostly German-speaking **Bernese uplands (Berner Oberland)**, arguably the best-known Alpine region, with famous places like Grindelwald and Lauterbrunnen and home of the awe-inspiring Eiger north face and the train that pierces through the mountain up to the Jungfraujoch at 3454m.

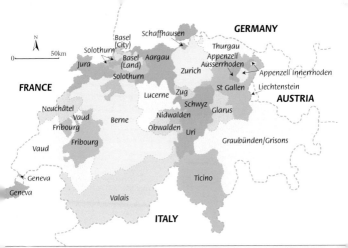

Lowest point: Lago Maggiore (193m).

Largest glacier: Aletsch in the Valais, with a surface area of 117km²/73mi²; 24km/15mi long. Total number of glaciers: 140

Largest lakes: Lake Geneva: 60% belongs to Switzerland (580km²/223mi²) and 40% to France. About 72km long and 14km wide at its widest point; Lake Constance: 536km²/208mi² (part belongs to Germany); Lake Neuchâtel: 215km²/83mi² — largest lake entirely on Swiss soil. Lakes in total: 1484

Highest freefalling waterfall: Staubbach Falls (Bernese Oberland), 300m/1000ft

Highest mountain road passes: Umbrail (between Grisons and Italy), 2501m; Nufenen (between the Valais and Ticino), 2478m; Great St-Bernard (between the Valais and Aosta in Italy), 2469m.

Largest dams: Grande Dixence (285m/935ft high, 700m/765yds long, retains 400m m³ water); Mauvoisin (250m/820ft high, 520m/570yds long, retains 211m m³ water)

UNESCO World Heritage Sites: nine sites as of 2008 (six cultural and three natural), among them the Jungfrau/Aletsch/Bietschhorn (2001 and 2007, natural site); Lavaux, Vineyard Terraces (2007, cultural site)

• The **Valais**, the third largest canton, situated in the southwest of Switzerland and cradling the Rhône Valley. The upper valley is German-, the lower valley French-speaking (the language border is the Raspille stream between Sierre and Salgesch). The Valais is a region of contrasts. The main Rhône Valley is warm and sunny, with orchards full of apples, pears, peaches and apricots, and terraced vineyards on the slopes. But hidden away in the side-valleys, some of Europe's highest mountains and largest glaciers tower up. There is hardly a valley without a dam, some of which have mammoth dimensions that leave you in utter disbelief and amazement. Valais is also home to world-famous skiing resorts — Zermatt (Matterhorn country), Crans-Montana and Verbier.

Getting there and getting about

The easiest way to travel to Western Switzerland is by **air**. The largest airports are Zurich and Geneva, and both are served by low-cost carriers. From the airport you can easily hop onto public transport. At time of writing, there are also budget flights to Basel-Mulhouse and Berne. Car rental, available at all the airports and in most large towns, can be pre-booked as a fly/drive deal. There are also local car rental companies, which may be cheaper. Do not discount package holidays — there is plenty of choice to many of the resorts.

But it's also easy to travel from the UK to Switzerland by **train**. You can get from London to Paris in just 2h15min with Eurostar, then transfer to a high-speed TGV to Geneva, for a relaxing and pleasant 3h30min ride. If you're not staying in or near Geneva, the trains will take you just where you *are* staying. Just look at the website www.seat61.com for a mouth-watering selection of options, outlined in great detail by a rail enthusiast.

Driving to Western Switzerland is an option and is recommended for those who enjoy the flexibility and freedom of having their own transport. After crossing the English Channel by either tunnel or ferry (there are also ferries from Hull and Rosyth in Scotland to Zeebrugge) it is an easy day's drive to Geneva. Unfortunately, there are *no* motorail services to Switzerland. Be aware that to drive on the Swiss motorways you must purchase a 'Vignette' (motorway tax sticker). At press date these cost £21 if purchased before you leave (contact Switzerland Tourism; www.myswitzerland.com), or 40CHF if bought on the spot at the border. Vignettes are valid from 1 December of the year prior to that printed on the sticker through to 31 January of the year following that printed on the sticker.

PUBLIC TRANSPORT IN SWITZERLAND

Switzerland has arguably the world's best public transport system. If there is one country in the world where you can explore a vast majority of its mountain land-scape by public transport, it is Switzerland. Where trains (see pages 56-63) don't go, buses will — even to remote valleys and hamlets (see www.postauto.ch), honking their melodious and famous theme from the overture of Rossini's *William Tell* as they wind up the mountain passes (to get you in the mood, there's a soundtrack at www.post.ch/de/pag-nat-posthorn.mp3).

Routes in the country — rail, bus, cable car, funicular and boat can be seen on one downloadable map: go to www.swisstravelsystem.com and click on services, then 'Synoptic map'. It even indicates the validity of the various tickets.

Railways

The Swiss Federal Railways have an excellent website which contains train, bus, boat, cable car, gondolas and funiculars routes including most of those operated by privately-owned companies (www.sbb.ch; English version available; (0900 300 300 from anywhere in Switzerland).

If you live outside Switzerland

Any non-resident of Switzerland or the Principality of Liechtenstein is entitled to buy the passes for the Swiss Travel System (www.swisstravelsystem.ch) described below. No photo is required; a valid passport or identity card is sufficient. The choice is somewhat bewildering, but you can tailor your holidays and take advantage of a network of 20,000km of train, bus and boat routes. These passes are also available through your local travel agency.

• **Swiss Pass:** allows unlimited travel on Swiss Travel System's public transport network during either 4, 8, 15 or 22 *consecutive* days or one full month. It includes the public transport systems of 38 Swiss cities and gives a 50% discount on most mountaintop trains and cable cars, plus free entry to some 450 museums. *The Swiss Pass is the most popular transport ticket.*

• **Swiss Flexi Pass:** allows travellers to choose their days of travel to suit themselves. You may travel on the Swiss Travel System network for 3, 4, 5 or 6 *non-consecutive* days within a month; on the days you select, you have all the same options as when travelling with a Swiss Pass. On the days between the first and the last validated day, your Swiss Flexi Pass offers a 50%

discount on train, (post) bus and boat trips, as well as on most mountaintop railways and cable cars.

• **Swiss Saver Pass/Swiss Saver Flexi Pass**: if two or more people travelling together buy either of the above passes, each receives a 15% discount.

• **Swiss Youth Pass**: those under 26 years of age can obtain a Swiss Youth Pass at a 25% discount on the full fare. Exactly the same advantages are offered as for the full Swiss Pass.

• **Swiss Transfer Ticket:** includes one free return trip to anywhere in Switzerland. The trip can start either at the Swiss border or at any Swiss airport. It is valid for up to a month. Each trip must be completed by the end of the day and has to be as direct as possible. These tickets are the ideal solution if you are only staying for a brief period (and not moving about) — or for winter holidays, where you just want to get to one destination and stay put. The Swiss Transfer Ticket is *not available in Switzerland,* but only at foreign sales points and from the on-line ticket shop at www.swisstravelsystem.ch.

'Chocolate-box' hamlets are within reach by post bus or mountaintop railway; this is on the way from Grosse Scheidegg to Grindelwald (Alternative walk 17), with the Fiescher Glacier in the upper half of the photograph and Lower Grindelwald Glacier in the lower half..

• **Swiss Card**: includes the first and last trip from the border or airport to one's destination and back, and also offers a 50% discount on all trips by train, lake boat, (post) bus and most mountain trains and cable cars between these first and last trips. It is valid for one month but, once the included return has been used, it is no longer valid. The first and last trip must be completed by the end of the day, and each trip must be as direct as possible. This offer is a good idea if you are staying in one region the entire time and just going on local trips. The Swiss Card is available at foreign sales points, at the Swiss border, at airport railway stations, and from the on-line ticket shop mentioned above.

• **Swiss Half Fare Card**: valid for one month, it enables you to obtain a 50% discount on trains, buses, boats and most mountain trains and cable cars. It is ideal for shorter trips and excursions, in particular if these include mountain trains and cable cars. The Swiss Half Fare Card is available at most railway stations in Switzerland, many European travel agencies, and from the on-line ticket shop mentioned above.

• **Swiss Travel System Family Card**: if you have children, ask for a *free* Swiss Travel System Family Card. It will entitle your children under 16 years of age to free travel, as long as at least one parent accompanies them. Non-family members between the ages of 6 and 16 receive a 50% discount on all Swiss Travel System tickets.

If you live in Switzerland

• **Half Fare Card**: you pay only half the ordinary fare for train, bus and boat tickets, as well as for travel on most private rail networks and mountain railways. You choose the length of validity — it can be one, two or three years. Most residents of Switzerland have a half fare card.

• **General Abonnement (GA)**: gives residents unlimited travel on SBB's network as well as on most privately-operated railways. The card also entitles you to free travel on post buses, lake and river boats, and on trams and buses in numerous Swiss cities and urban networks. Many mountain railways and cable cars also grant special discounts for GA holders.

✿ Car touring

The car tours have been designed to show you the best of each area, with plenty of **short walks** where you can stretch your legs: there are 36 short walks especially for motorists, set apart from the main text by green lines and shown on the touring maps with the symbol ⊜.

The **touring maps** (with key to the symbols in the text) include all the places visited, but I suggest that you also obtain a good large-scale map such as 'Suisse romande' (1:200,000), available at eg petrol stations.

A few guidelines: the **speed limit** on motorways is 120km/h (usually reduced to 100km/h in tunnels); on cantonal roads 80km/h; in urban areas 50km/h. *Speed limits are strictly enforced*, with numerous radars. **Safety belts** are compulsory. There are plenty of **petrol stations**; if unstaffed, they can usually be used with credit cards. The **blood alcohol limit** is 0.05% (50mg/100ml, lower than in the UK). **Parking** is usually metered, so have change with you. A few villages are **car-free**. For all hikes, I recommend where to park. Many **mountain passes** are closed for traffic in winter; in the Jura most stay open throughout the year except for days of heavy snowfall, when you would need snow tires.

Narrow mountain roads may prove nerve-racking for some motorists. For cars of similar type, the car driving *uphill* has priority, unless a lay-by close at hand allows the driver to make way for the downhill motorist. Otherwise, heavier vehicles have priority over lighter ones. On postal mountain roads (road signs with a yellow horn on blue background), post buses have priority. *Toot when you can't see round the bend!*

Lake Geneva's wine region of Lavaux (Car tour 1 and Walk 4)

12

Car tour 1 (Lake Geneva): LAVAUX WINE ROUTE ABOVE THE SWISS RIVIERA

Lausanne-Ouchy • Lutry • Châtelard • Aran • Grandvaux •
Riex • Epesses • Chexbres • Vevey • Mont Pèlerin • Chexbres

38km/24mi; 1h driving
En route: Walks 4, 5, 6; additional short walk suggested below
Note: The scale of the touring map is too small to do justice to this tour,
but the maps for Walk 5 show most of the roads and villages in detail.

Dashing through the vineyards on the motorway high above Lake Geneva or even driving along the lake from Lausanne to Vevey won't allow you truly to absorb the splendid wine region of Lavaux, a UNESCO World Heritage Site. But there *is* a route which allows you to roam at a leisurely pace through the lanes of the wine growing villages, stop and enjoy the magnificent views, visit the cellars of the wine-growers, sample (and buy) the local wine, and even ramble through the vineyards. The slopes are steep; monorails and helicopters are used to get the grapes out of the vineyards. (It's best to avoid this route during the grape harvest, as agricultural vehicles block the already-narrow roads.) A side-trip leads you through fields, pastures and forest to the foot of Mont Pèlerin, a mountain above Vevey; from its tower there is a beautiful 360-degree view.

Starting at the port in **Lausanne-Ouchy** on Lake Geneva, follow the lakeside road towards VEVEY, via the suburbs **Pully** (1.2km), **Paudex** (3.5km) and **Lutry** (4km), all of which belong to metropolitan Lausanne.

Wine and vineyards

The Swiss like to drink their own wine. Only 1-2% of Switzerland's wine is exported. Viticulture is thriving, and quality and standards are high. About 50 grape varieties are planted on 15,000 ha. Some grapes are known internationally, others are grown only locally.

Of the whites, by far the most widely grown variety is the Chasselas (called Fendant in the Valais), followed by Müller-Thurgau, Chardonnay, Silvaner (Johannisberg). Of the reds, Pinot Noir is the clear number one, followed by Gamay. The popular Dôle is 80% a blend of Pinot Noir and Gamay grapes, with the remaining 20% coming from other varieties.

In Western Switzerland, wines are grown in the cantons of Valais, Vaud, Neuchâtel and Geneva. Wine regions offer some of the most beautiful walks in Switzerland. This guide includes four vineyard trails: in the Geneva hinterland (Walk 2), along Lake Geneva on the sloping hills of La Côte (Walk 3), in the fabulous Lavaux region with its steeply terraced vineyards (Walk 4), and in the Valais (Walk 21).

About 1.5km after you have entered Lutry (just before the Honda dealer at the corner on the left-hand side of the road; 5.5km), turn left towards GRANDVAUX, CHEXBRES (there is also a sign ROUTE DE VIGNOBLE). After 300m go underneath the railway bridge and then pass through the hamlet of **Châtelard** (6km). You are now in wine country. Proceed to **Aran** (7km; parking at the village entrance) and **Grandvaux** (town sign at 7.5km). At the junction in Grandvaux (7.7km), take the middle of three roads leading off to the right, towards CHEXBRES.

At the next roundabout, continue straight ahead into **Riex** (9.5km) and then **Epesses** (10.2km). The village roads are often very narrow; in Epesses, through traffic is regulated by traffic lights. At the end of Epesses there is a picnic area with benches (☐ 10.8km); there is parking about 200m further on, at a lay-by on the right (the parking spaces on the left just past the picnic area are usually occupied). About 1.5km after Epesses stop at a lay-by with an orientation table (☐) and a gorgeous view over outlandishly steep vineyards.

Enter **Chexbres**, the largest town in the Lavaux area. Turn right on the main street (13.5km) and continue through the town. Follow the road downhill towards VEVEY. About 700m after you have gone under the railway bridge in Chexbres, there is lay-by with an orientation table (☐). Descend all the way to the shore of the lake, merge with the main road coming from Lausanne (17km), go through **Corseaux** and enter **Vevey** (19km).

At the first roundabout in Vevey, take the exit three-quarters of the way around for MONT PELERIN/CHATEL-ST-DENNIS. The road climbs again. At the next roundabout (20km), again go three-quarters of the way around. The road rises in large zigzags (lay-by on the right 800m after the roundabout). At the third hairpin bend (22.5km), you have a choice: you can either branch off left here and go straight back to Chexbres via **Chardonne**, or you can continue the tour, exploring an entirely different landscape which surrounds the Mont Pèlerin area.

For the latter, after the third hairpin bend, go through **Jongny** (23km) and continue towards CHATEL-ST-DENNIS. Turn left 2km further on for PLEIN CIEL/MT PELERIN; 25km) and after barely 1km go sharp left. In the distance you can see the tower on Mont Pèlerin. The road takes you back into Jongny (26.5km) and through the village of **Mont Pèlerin** (27.5km), then rises before dropping slightly. Bear right (30km) and drive up the narrow road to the parking area (975m; 31.5km) almost on the top of **Mont Pèlerin**.

Short walk: Mont Pèlerin (2km, 45min, ascent 110m) From the parking area, follow the surfaced road (barred to traffic) to the forest-covered summit of **Mont Pèlerin** (1080m) with its 'Plein Ciel' TV tower (♦ open Apr-Oct, 9.00-18.00). When visibility is good, take the outside see-through lift to the top and enjoy a 360-degree view. To return, you can cut some loops off the road: take the forest trail waymarked in blue: it starts just a few paces from the revolving door of the Mont Pèlerin compound. Follow this to the BUVETTE DU DEFIRAN (café-restaurant), then take a surfaced road back to the parking area.

Go back down the same road for 1.5km (33km) and turn right, driving past farm houses and through the hamlet of **Cremières** (35km) towards CHEXBRES. When you meet a road, turn right (*no signs;* 37.5km). After a few hundred metres you can either take the motorway back to Lausanne or return to **Chexbres**.

Car tour 2 (Jura and Lake Geneva):
SOUTHERN JURA AND LA COTE

Nyon • St-Cergue • Arzier • Marchissy • St-George • Col du Marchairuz • Le Brassus • Lac de Joux • Le Pont • Dent de Vaulion • Romainmôtier • La Sarraz • Cossonay • Cottens • Bussy • Aubonne • Mont-sur-Rolle • Nyon

129km/80mi; 2h30min driving
En route: Walks 3, 7, 8; additional short walks suggested below

Driving in the Jura, undulating through forests and grassy pastures, with views of Lake Geneva, this tour also takes you to the largest lake in the Swiss Jura mountain range, the Lac de Joux. The last part of the drive leads through the wine country on the sloping hills above Lake Geneva called La Côte.

Start from **Nyon**, or exit 11 (0km) on the Lausanne/ Geneva motorway. Follow signs to ST-CERGUE. The road is pretty straight for about 3.5km, but then starts snaking up through the Jura woodlands. After 10.5km there is a parking area on the left-hand side of the road (take care, it's just before a hairpin bend) with a nice view over the lake

and towards the Mont Blanc massif (⌕🍴). Continue to **St-Cergue** (1047m; 12km), a small summer and winter resort. The main tour goes straight on at the roundabout here, but you could get to the starting point of Walk 7 by turning left at this roundabout, towards LA CURE; it's 4km to the start.
Continuing straight on, you

reach **Arzier** (17km). About 200m after the first railway crossing in this village, a parking area with benches on the left-hand side of the road offers a lovely view of the Alps (☞). When you cross the railway tracks for the second time, turn left after 200m onto a narrower road. Go through **Bassins** and **Le Vaud** to arrive at a junction (26km). Drive straight ahead uphill, passing through the villages of **Marchissy**, **Longirod** and coming into **St-George** (30km). Turn left in this village, towards the COL DU MARCHAIRUZ. After 5km turn left at the junction; 1.8km further on, a parking area on the right offers a fine view, but for a short walk drive another 300m to a second parking area, on the left.

Short walk: Sentier du Sapin à Siméon (1.7km, 30min, ascent 70m; 7 information panels). This

beautiful stroll takes you across mountain pastures dotted about the Jura forest, with pleasant views to Lake Geneva and the Alps. Cross the main road and walk up the asphalted path for seven minutes, then turn right on the gravel path. After you have crossed the main road a second time, take a look at the orientation table opposite the first parking area. Notice the restored stone walls, many of which were built hundreds of years ago to delineate boundaries and confine cattle.

Just 1.5km past the parking area you are on the **Col du Marchairuz** (1447m, 38km, ⛰ www.hotel-marchairuz.ch). This pass, with a parking area, is one of the starting points for tackling Mont Tendre, the highest mountain in the Swiss Jura (see Walk 8 and photograph overleaf).

On the descent from the pass there are various parking places at the right or left of the road. In the winter, this is a very popular cross-country skiing and snowshoe area. In **Le Brassus** (1036m, 45km) turn right towards LE PONT. For the next 12km the road is quite straight and leads along the shore of the **Lac de Joux**, the largest lake in the Swiss Jura at an altitude of about 1000m. The mountain falling off steeply at the northern end of the lake is La Dent de Vaulion (see the short walk on page 19).

You need not go all the way into Le Pont if you just want to stretch your legs beside the lake for a short time. You

Sunflower fields in the Geneva hinterland, with the southern Swiss Jura in the background

could park about 1km before Le Pont, in a parking area on the left a few hundred metres past the village of **L'Abbaye**. (And if you already know that you won't be stopping in Le Pont, then fork right for the *COL DU MOLLENDRUZ* at the junction in L'Abbaye.)

The main tour goes into **Le Pont** (59km), at the north-eastern tip of the lake, from where you can take the short walk below. If you are not stopping here, you must make

a *very sharp* U-turn to the right at the entrance to Le Pont, towards the *COL DU MOLLEN-DRUZ* — so sharp that you might find it easier to keep *left* (watching out traffic from the right as you do so!) and turn round somewhere in the village to get back to this junction.)

Short walk: Shore of *Lac de Joux* (as far/long as you like, hardly any height gain). Stop in **Le Pont**. There is parking on the left just where you enter the village and a larger parking area at the far end, by the railway station. The entire distance from Le Pont to the far southwestern end of the lake is about 9km, but you can just skirt the shore for as long as you like. In winter, you can even walk on the lake itself, since it's usually frozen over.

Heading from Le Pont towards the Col du Mollen-

House in Romainmôtier

druz, after about 2.5km turn left at a junction (for VAULION, ABBATIALE DE ROMAINMOTIER). After another 4km (65km) you could take a 9km return detour to the left, following signposting for DENT DE VAULION.

Short walk: Dent de Vaulion

(1km, 30min, ascent 80m). The **Dent de Vaulion** (1483m, orientation table) has a marvellous sweeping view to the east across the Alpine chain and to the southwest over the Lac de Joux and the adjacent Lac Brenet. It can be reached on foot from Le Pont in 1h30min, but there's an easier ascent — you can drive almost to the top. Follow the signposted road past the Auberge du Morez (🍴), beyond which the road gets very narrow. You are allowed to drive all the way up to the parking area

at the CHALET DE LA DENT DE VAULION (1410m, 🍴 open mid-May to end Oct). From here it's just a 15-minute walk to the summit.

The main tour continues ahead via **Vaulion** to **Romainmôtier** (74km). At the end of this village turn sharp right, to descend to the picturesque old centre (car park 200m outside). The famous Romanesque abbey is worth a visit (⛪ church open daily 8.00-19.00).
Head back to the junction and continue the tour via **Croy**. Immediately after this village you join a wide road towards LAUSANNE, by turning left and then making a U-turn to the right. Turn right in **La Sarraz** (84km ⛪) towards NYON/ AUBONNE. In **Cossonay** (89km) bear right for AUBONNE. You now go through a string of villages — Senarclens (96km), Granzy, Cottens, Clarmont, Bussy and Lavigny; en route you catch glimpses of Lake Geneva again, and vineyards start to pop up.
When you reach **Aubonne** (107km), follow the *blue-signposted* road for GENEVA (green signposting denotes the motorway). In **Féchy** (110km) there is a small parking area on the right-hand side of the road from where you could walk up to the pretty village of Féchy Dessus in less than 10 minutes. Now you traverse the vineyard region of **La Côte** (Walk 3), going through **Mont-sur-Rolle**, Bursins, Vinzel, Luins, Vich and Prangin before arriving at **Nyon** (126km).
The motorway is 3km away.

View from the top of Mont Tendre (Walk 8)

Car tour 3 (Jura): VAL DE TRAVERS AND LAKE NEUCHATEL

Yverdon-les-Bains • Vuiteboeuf • Ste-Croix • Col des Etroits • Fleurier • Môtiers • Couvet • Travers • Noiraigue • Rochefort • Corselle • Neuchâtel • Auvernier • Colombier • Boudry • Bevaix • Gorgier • Vaumarcus • Concise • Grandson • Yverdon-les-Bains

100km/62mi or more (depending on route); 2h driving
En route: Walks 9, 10; additional short walks suggested below

This is a tour full of contrasts. First we explore the sylvan Jura, with suggested excursions into the tight gorges of Covatanne, Poëta Raisse and Areuse — or onto one of its highest points, Le Chasseron. Then we visit the wine country on the sloping hills of the Jura, following the shore of Lake Neuchâtel and enjoying sweeping views across the lake to the Alpine chain.

Take Exit 2 (OUEST) off the A5 motorway at **Yverdon-les-Bains** (0km) and follow signposting to STE-CROIX. A first stop is suggested in the village of **Vuiteboeuf** (7km).

Short walk: Covatanne Gorge
(1.5km, 30min, ascent 70m; 4.2km, 1h30min, ascent 280m; or 11.5km, 2h15min, ascent 420m). Just before leaving **Vuiteboeuf**, a few metres before you cross the bridge over the **Arnon River**, there's a parking

area on the left in a former quarry (600m). Take the ascending path just before the bridge, immediately penetrating the **Covatanne Gorge**. After 15 minutes, a wide path branching off to the right leads to a couple of benches about 100m from the junction, an inviting picnic spot. Go back to the junction and either return to Vuiteboeuf (for the shortest option), or continue the climb through the ever-narrowing gorge. After 50 minutes (880m) you leave the gorge. If you want to continue further, climb another 15 minutes, to arrive at the bypass road for the hamlet **Le Château** (1000m). Turn right and follow the road for about 100m, then take the signposted path descending to the right. After 15 minutes, at a junction, take the path with a brown sign, *VOIE HISTORIQUE*, climbing for a few more minutes. You pass a couple of places where wheel tracks dating from the 14th century are clearly visible carved in the rocks; they were used until 1760 to keep the waggons on this salt

In the Covatanne Gorge

route on the track. While you are comfortably crossing mountain passes in your car or by train, think of all the hue and cry of the waggoners as they crossed the mountain with their goods. On the descent, the trail crosses the road several times before arriving back in **Vuiteboeuf**.

After Vuiteboeuf the road starts its steep climb to the small town of Ste-Croix, eased by numerous hairpin bends. **Ste-Croix** (18km) may well be the world's music box centre, and there are two museums devoted to this craft: the Music Box and Automata Museum (CIMA, Centre International de la Méchanique d'Art), 100m off the main road to the left (**M** open Tue-Sun 13.30-18.00, Mon and mornings on request), and the family-run Musée Baud in L'Auberson, 4km from Ste-Croix (a detour down to the left from the Col des Etroits, where the main tour goes right).
Northeast of Ste-Croix is **Le Chasseron** (1607m; ▲▲), one of the highest peaks in the Swiss Jura, from where you have a 360-degree view and can admire the entire chain of the Alps (see also Walk 9).

Short walk: Le Chasseron (5km, 2h, ascent 410m or 1.5km, 35min, ascent 120m). In Ste-Croix, turn right and drive to the hamlet of Les Rasses, a small ski station. Turn left in **Les Rasses** for CHASSERON and park in the large parking area. Follow the walkers' signs to LE CHASSERON. The first 10 minutes are on the ski slopes, then the trail branches off to the right and goes through forest. After 45 minutes the tree line is reached. You cross meadows to the HOTEL DU CHASSERON, only a few metres below the summit. Return the same way.
For the shorter version, continue driving past the car park in Les Rasses; the narrow, winding road rises to just below the tree line at 1440m. There are two parking areas, 100m apart, beyond which cars are not normally allowed (except for the elderly/disabled, in bad weather, or after 18.00). Walk across pastures to the summit and back.

Just past Ste-Croix, on the **Col des Etroits** (1166m), turn right and descend the narrow **Vallon de Noirvaux** to **Fleurier** (31km). From here the main tour turns right for MOTIERS, but if you would like a short walk (or drive) to a fine viewpoint over the Val de Travers, first turn *left* towards PONTPARLIER and, just after crossing the railway line, park at the large parking area on the right-hand side of the road, if you plan to walk to the viewpoint. Otherwise, drive on to the main road to Pontparlier. Go left and, shortly after, left again (signed to ST-SULPICE). At the end of St-Sulpice, drive up the narrow road signposted to the CHAPEAU NAPOLEON.

Short walk: Chapeau de Napoléon (2.3km, 1h or 5km, 1h40min, ascent 220m). Follow the signs to CHAPEAU NAPOLEON. The ascent is fairly strenuous, but 35 minutes should see you to the top (✕ with fine views and 5-room ▲: (032 861 16 62, www.chapeaudenapoleon.ch). If you don't want to go back the same way (1h), walk to **St-Sulpice**, then follow the roadside pavement back to **Fleurier** (1h40min).

Steps and waterfall in the Poëta Raisse Gorge (Walk 9)

The next village en route is **Môtiers** (34km). In the centre a road goes off right and leads after 1.1km to a parking area, the starting point of Walk 9 through the gorge of Poëta Raisse, another of the Jura's impressive gorges.

Short walk: Poëta Raisse. See page 103 — you can choose **Shorter walk 9-1** (6.5km, 2h45min, ascent 380m) or **Shorter walk 9-2** (7km, 2h10min, ascent 300m).

Continue from Môtiers to **Couvet** (36km). Before you

cross the railway line and bridge here, a road forks off right to the Creux du Van (see below and Walk 10). Between Couvet and Travers, you might like to take a road off right (signposted MINES D'ASPHALTE). This 1.4km return detour leads to **old asphalt mines**, in use from 1712 until 1986 (✕ open daily Apr-Oct, 10.30-14.30, ✆ 032 864 90 64). You can explore 1km; wear warm clothing — it's only 6°C underground. Back on the main road, travel through **Travers** and arrive in **Noiraigue** (45km). If you'd like to try Short walk 10-1 to the Creux du Van — the most visited and most natural attraction in the Swiss Jura — take the road off right in the village centre, signposted to the FERME (farm) ROBERT (a gite d'étape). Otherwise continue on the main road, which now starts to climb.

Short walk: Areuse Gorge (4km, 1h30min, ascent 100m). After Noiraigue, between **Brot-Dessous** and Rochefort, a narrow road branches off right (a

Walk 10: on the plateau of the Creux du Van in winter

U-bend turning) and descends to the hamlet **Champ du Moulin-Dessous**, the starting point for Walk 10. **Shorter walk 10-2** is an easy stroll to the gorge with its romantic bridge, shown on page 107. The walk can be continued to **Noiraigue**, from where you can take the train back to Champ du Moulin.

Continue on the main road to **Rochefort** (54km) and from there go straight on. The view widens out — you can see Lake Neuchâtel and the Alps. Pass through **Corselle** and follow signposting to **Neuchâtel** (pop 32,000; 64km).

Short walk along the shore of Lake Neuchâtel (from 30min to 16.6km/4h20min if going all the way to Bevaix). A beautiful *Sentier du Lac* (lakeside walk) runs from Neuchâtel to Bevaix. Almost the entire walk is along the shore; signposting is good, and you can't go wrong. From **Neuchâtel to Bevaix** allow about 4h, plus 20 minutes and 60m in height gain from the lake to the centre and railway station. But you can also do just parts of the walk — for instance from Neuchâtel (Place Pury with underground garage next to the Hôtel Beaurivage) to **Auvernier** (see text at the right for parking places), or from **Auvernier to Colombier**, or the stroll between the shore of the lake and vineyard hills that starts in **Petit Cortaillod** (turn left before Boudry; parking area).

The route from Neuchâtel to Yverdon-les-Bains leads through wine country on the sloping hills of the Jura, with fine views to the lake and the chain of the Alps. A long line of castles stretches along Lake Neuchâtel — almost every village has its own castle. You have a choice of three routes for this drive. (1) Take the A5 motorway (green signs; 100km); although there *are* some nice views, tunnels and walls limit visibility. (2) The main road A5 (blue signs) often runs parallel with the motorway, but offers somewhat better vistas. (3) If you like a pinch of adventure, take the wine route (*Route de Vignobles*, abbreviated *RdV* in this description), a combination of the main A5 road and secondary roads higher up above the lake (*which are very narrow in places*).

Note that there is no single 'wine route'; all stretches of road that pass by scenic vineyards or go to wine cellars are labelled as such. Signposting is quite good (although the *RdV* logo changes format about halfway along, when you enter a different canton). For this route, leave Neuchâtel and follow the signs for LAUSANNE, then AUVERNIER. Just after the village sign for **Auvernier** there is a car park on your left. Auvernier is just a few metres from the lake and allows for strolling both along the shore (even though the nearby motorway is a bit noisy) and through the pleasing old village.

Next is **Colombier** (parking 'Plage' at the left of the main road). The castle here hosts a military museum (■M open Mar-Oct, Tue-Fri, 14.00-17.00; also open on the first Sun of each month at 15.00; (032 889 54 99, www. military.ch/EIM).

Follow signs to BOUDRY. In **Boudry**, leave the through

a detour here by forking right, up to the castle (🏛 visits only by appointment; mobile 079 698 69 08; www. chateauvaumarcus.ch; ✗ with a fine view).

Back on the main A5 road, follow the RdV SIGN. You are now entering the region called **Coteaux** (hillside) **de Bonvillars**. Just before Concise the battlefield of Grandson lies 1.5km off the main road (there is a memorial stone and an information panel in French and German, but nowhere to park). All Swiss schoolchildren learn about the three greatest battles ever won by a Swiss army. One such battle was the Battle of Grandson (see below) in 1476.

Continue through **Concise**, **Corcelles** and **Onnens**. After Onnens, turn right (RdV SIGN) at the roundabout in the middle of fields, heading straight towards the Jura and driving through **Bonvillars**. After **Champagne**, follow the signposting for *GRANDSON* (*don't* follow the RdV sign by the motorway — this would take you back the way you've just come). In **Grandson**, stop to visit the castle — one of the largest fortresses in Switzerland and home to — among other things — a museum of arms, a layout of the Battle of Grandson, a torture chamber and a display of the booty from 1476, as well as classic old cars. (🏛M open daily Apr-Oct, 08.30-18.00, Nov-Mar 08.30-17.00, ☎ 024 445 29 26, www.chateau-grandson.ch, 20-minute film show in English).

End the tour in **Yverdon-les-Bains** (pop 23,000), one of Switzerland's best-known spas.

road and turn *left* at the Hôtel de Lion d'Or (*don't* turn right even though the *RdV* sign points to the right). This one-way cobblestone street goes up through the picturesque old village of Boudry. Stop at the first parking area and walk back a couple of hundred metres to visit the wine and viticulture museum — accommodated in, of course, a castle (**M** open Wed-Sun, 14.00-18.00, ☎ 032 842 10 98, www. chateaudeboudry.ch).

After Boudry, you are back on the main A5 road to Bevaix. Turn right in the village of **Bevaix** (*RdV* SIGN). Once past Bevaix's small railway station on your left, the road narrows as it runs through the residential area, then through forest. Leaving the forest, bear left for *GORGIER*. This is a scenic stretch, with beautiful views of the Alps and the lake. Descending into a gorge, suddenly the private castle of **Gorgier** rises just in front of you as the narrow road swings round it. Drive through Gorgier and the adjacent villages of **St-Aubin** and **Sauges**. The road descends to **Vaumarcus**. You could take

Car tour 4 (Jura): NORTHERN JURA WITH MOUNT WEISSENSTEIN

Solothurn • Mount Weissenstein • Crémines • Moutier • Delémont • Col des Rangiers • St-Ursanne • Col de la Croix • Charmoille • Movelier • Soyhières • Laufen • Breitenbach • Passwang • Scheltenpass • Mervelier • Vermes • Crémines • Welschenrohr • Balsthal • Oensingen • Solothurn

215km/133mi; 4-5h driving
En route: Walk 12; additional short walks suggested below

This circuit leads through the northern part of the Jura. Wide valleys, narrow gorges and rolling hills interspersed with forest and lush meadows characterize the bucolic countryside. The driving is somewhat taxing — you will cross five passes (Weissenstein, Col des Rangiers, Col de la Croix, Passwang, Scheltenpass) — but the views, near and far, are spectacular.

Take exit 41 (*SOLOTHURN*) off the A1 motorway, to join the A5 motorway. Then leave the A5 at exit 33 (*SOLOTHURN-OST*) and follow the signs for *SOLOTHURN*, then *BIEL/BIENNE*. Cross the wide **Aare River** (0km), with the old town of Solothurn and its landmark, the St Ursen Cathedral, on the left. **Solothurn** (pop 15,000; ♣M) is Switzerland's most baroque town — its old centre is a gem not to be missed. The superb Fine Arts Museum (Kunstmuseum), Natural History Museum (Natur-museum) and Old Arsenal (Altes Zeughaus) are all in the old town. There are three large underground car parks just outside the old town (Baseltor, Bieltor and Berntor).

From Solothurn follow signs to *WEISSENSTEIN*. Pass through the small town of **Langendorf** (3km) on the outskirts of Solothurn, followed by **Ober-dorf** (4km ♟). If you are going to Walk 12, Oberdorf's chairlift station is about 1km outside the village. The road up **Mount Weissenstein** (snow-free from around April to December) is *steep*, with a gradient of up to 22%. Almost at the top, take the small road just past the restaurant Senn-haus (10km) on your right (no sign). After just 200m you reach the car park for the Kur-haus Weissenstein (▲ ✕ ☕). Walk the few metres to the hotel's terrace and enjoy a marvelous panorama, visibility permitting (orientation table).

Short walk: from the Kurhaus Weissenstein to Röti and back

(3.5km, 1h, ascent 170m). From the hotel terrace, head east on an undulating path (signposted) which rises to the highest peak of the Weissenstein range, **Röti** (1395m). Take in the panoramic view and return the same way.

Return to the main road and, 0.5km past the Sennhaus Restaurant, you will reach the **Weissenstein Pass** (1279m) amidst trees. The gradient of the *narrow road downhill* is up to 15%. When the mountain road merges with cantonal route 30 (15km), turn left. Running along a narrow gorge, this road takes you through the hamlet of **Gäns-brunnen** and the villages of

Crémines (19km) and Grandval, then the outskirts of Belprahon and Eschert. The **La Raus** stream is on your left and the railway on your right. Go under a bridge and straight on into **Moutier** (24km), a small industrial town famous for its Monk's Head cheese (Tête de Moine).

In Moutier turn right towards DELEMONT. Between Moutier and Delémont, the road runs parallel with the **Birse River** which created the narrow canyon. You pass through the villages of **Roches**, **Choindez** and **Courrendlin** before reaching Delémont in an open plain. **Delémont** (pop 12,000; 39km) is the capital of Jura, Switzerland's youngest canton, created in 1979. Head towards the old town (there are car parks just outside) and take a stroll. Two gates dating from the Middle Ages and parts of the town walls remain.

Short walk: *Chapelle du Vorbourg* in Delémont (1.2km, 30min, 70m ascent). Following the sign VORBOURG from the northeastern tip of the old town, drive up through a residential area to the **Chapelle du Vorbourg** on a wooded ledge amidst forest (if you walk, 2km from the old town; 40min, 100m ascent). About 200m before the chapel, *don't* take the road branching off right to the chapel (no parking space), but continue straight on. There is a parking area just a few metres after the junction. If it's full, continue along the narrow road for another 400m and park at the Restaurant Vorbourg (or along-side the road) at the end of the road. If you look up from the restaurant, you will see the remnants of an old CASTLE atop the

hill. Take the hiking path from the restaurant; it zigags up to the ruins. Descend on the other side of the hill, turn left at the first junction and right a few metres further on at the next junction. This takes you to the road, with a view of Delémont. Follow the road back to the restaurant, visiting the chapel on the way.

From Delémont's old town drive back to the railway station, then turn right and — once out of town — take the old road (*not* the motorway) towards PORRENTRUY. Heading west, you go through the village of **Develier** and cross the **Col des Rangiers** (856m; 52km; ✕). At a junction 1.4km down from the pass, turn left for ST-URSANNE. The road winds down into a narrow gorge. Pass under the viaduct, go straight on at the roundabout, cross the **river Doubs** and come to **St-Ursanne** (59km ▲✕🏠). The old town is on the far side of the river and can be reached via a footbridge. There are various car parks, some a fair way from the old town. St-Ursanne is a medieval pearl and one of the prettiest villages in the Jura. There are a few picnic tables along the river — or try to get a table on the terrace of the hotel-restaurant Demi-Lune next to the bridge and just above the river.

Short walk: *St-Ursanne* (2km, 45min, ascent 60m). This is a good way to work up an appetite — or work off a good lunch! Leave the old town by crossing the MEDIEVAL FOOTBRIDGE, and turn left. Walk along the pavement for 170m, then bear left and, after a further 130m, join a path running alongside the

The lovely setting of the Demi-Lune Hotel at St-Ursanne, just beside the medieval footbridge over the river Doubs

Doubs. Cross the river on the ROAD BRIDGE and at the roundabout turn left return on the roadside pavement back to the old town. About 150m after you enter the old town through the gate (main street 23 JUNE), look for CHEMIN DE LA CHAPELLE on your right, a small alley that doesn't seem to lead anywhere, but actually climbs up to a chapel. From there, take steps (190 of them) back down, to enter the old town through its other gate.

From St-Ursanne you could short-cut the main tour by driving back to Delémont and from there taking the road via Soyhières to Laufen (Laufon in French), rejoining the tour at the 113km-point.
The main tour now crosses the rolling hills of the Jura. From the footbridge in St-Ursanne continue for 1km on the left-hand side of the Doubs, then the road turns right to cross the river. At the roundabout, turn right and head back towards ST-URSANNE, but then take a sharp left, to drive up to the **Col de la Croix** (789m). Beyond this pass the tour runs

via the villages/hamlets of Courtemautruy (68km), **Courgenay** (where you turn right), **Cornol**, Fregiécourt, **Charmoille** and **Lucelle** (81km). Between Lucelle and **Ederswiler** (90km) you're never quite sure whether you're in France or Switzerland. Beyond **Movelier** you finally arrive in **Soyhières** (100km), where you turn left on the main road.
Follow this through a narrow valley to **Laufen** (113km), which also has a largely preserved old town. In Laufen turn right towards PASSWANG. Go through the villages of **Breitenbach** and adjacent Büsserach, then **Erschwil** and **Beinwil**, before tackling the **Passwang pass** (1025m; 133km). Almost at the top of this pass, the road makes a 90° bend to the right and immediately enters a tunnel. For a beautiful short walk, see the following description; otherwise, go through the tunnel.

Short walk: Passwang (5.4km, 2h, 300m ascent; can be shortened to 4km, 1h15min, 200m ascent). *Just a few metres* before the TUNNEL leave the main road and continue straight on (watching out for oncoming traffic emerging from the tunnel). Drive 500m and stop at a large parking area (alt 982m). From here follow the gently rising surfaced road past a farm (its restaurant is closed). At a FIRST PASS (1166m), turn right; in five minutes you reach a wonderful 360° viewpoint (1198m, sharp drop-off). If visibility is good — it is at its best in winter — you can see the Alps from Bavaria in Germany to France and, on the other side, the Vosges in France and the Black Forest in Germany. You can retrace your steps from here, but, for the longer version, continue along the ridge, enter the forest and come to the true summit of **Mount Passwang** (1204m) — where there is no view at all! Carry on another 500m to a junction, turn left and descend to the VOGELBERG RESTAURANT (1106m ✖). Another 60m in height gain now takes you back to the FIRST PASS (1166m); from there retrace your steps to the car park.

Out of the tunnel, zigzag down from the pass. If you stay on this road, you can cut short the tour by driving straight to Balsthal (the 192km-point), saving 56km. But the main tour turns sharp right 2.9km down from the pass towards SCHELTEN (136km; *this junction is easily missed*), to meander through beautiful Jura back-country on narrow, winding secondary roads, alternating between tight gorges and wide-open spaces. A stream, the **Guldentalbach**, is your companion until you start climbing to the **Scheltenpass** (1051m; 143km), from where

you descend beside the **Scheltenbach**, flowing in a narrow gorge.

Go through the villages of **Mervelier** (where the road widens out), Corban and **Courchapoix** (154km). About 2km after Courchapoix, turn left towards VERMES. Another narrow gorge takes you to **Vermes** (160km ♟), where you can admire the 15th-century frescos in the church. Then the road narrows again and winds uphill. At a junction, bear right. Drive through Corcelles and, in **Crémines** (171km), turn left and follow the road which you took earlier — but this time in the opposite direction. Pass Gänsbrunnen and continue back to Solo-thurn — either by tackling the Weissenstein Pass again or by continuing on the fairly straight canton route 30 to Balsthal.

If you choose the latter route, you will go through the village of **Welschenrohr** and the out-skirts of Herbetswil, Matzen-dorf and Laupersdorf. Once in **Balsthal** (192km), turn right at the roundabout and after 200m stop at the parking area and take the five-minute walk up to the clifftop castle of Alt Falkenstein (◼M of local history open Apr-Oct, Wed-Sun 14.00-17.00, Sat/Sun also 10.00-12.00, cl Mon/Tue, www.museum-alt-falkenstein. ch). There's a second castle, Neu Falkenstein (⬜), in the north of the town; you see it if you take the direct route from Passwang to Balsthal. Only ruins remain, as it fell victim to arson in 1798.

From Balsthal go on to OEN-SINGEN and from **Oensingen** (195km) take the motorway to return to **Solothurn** (215km).

Car tour 5: VAUD AND FRIBOURG ALPS

Aigle • Col des Mosses • L'Etivaz • Château-d'Oex • Rossinière • Montbovon • Gruyères • Broc • Charmey • Jaun • Jaunpass • Zweisimmen • Saanen • Gstaad • Gsteig • Col du Pillon • Les Diablerets • Col de la Croix • Villars-sur-Ollon • Ollon • Aigle

174km/108mi; 3h driving
En route: Walks 13, 14, 15; additional short walks suggested below

This tour explores the Alps of southern Vaud and northern Fribourg, as well as touching on the fringes of a third canton, Berne. These mountain heights are modest compared with the 4000m-high summits in the Valais: the highest mountain in the Fribourg Alps is grassy-rocky Vanil Noir at 2389m, and in the Vaud Alps rocky-icy Les Diablerets (3210m). But the scenery and opportunities for hiking on this tour are splendid.

The circuit starts in Aigle, a wine-producing centre in the foothills of the Vaud Alps, climbs to the Vaud highlands (Pays d'Enhaut) with the villages L'Etivaz (cheese), Château-d'Oex, Rougemont and Rossinière, and moves on to the Gruyère region (more cheese), which is the centre of the Fribourg Alps. Next you enter the canton of Berne, climbing across the Jaun Pass and visiting the quiet small towns of Zweisimmen and Saanen, the village of Gsteig and the glamorous resort of Gstaad. Back in the Vaud Alps, you cross the Pillon Pass with the towering Les Diablerets massif as backdrop, and an even higher pass, the Col de la Croix, before the long descent leads back to Aigle.

The pretty church at Rossinière is a lovely place for a picnic, with views over Lake Vernex and to the surrounding mountains.

There are various ways to shorten the tour:

(1) Southern part of the Vaud Alps only: halfway between Aigle and the Col des Mosses, turn right towards COL DU PILLON and drive to the village of Les Diablerets, then follow the main tour from the 140km-point back to Aigle. 53km; 1h15min driving.

(2) Vaud Alps only: from Aigle follow the main tour to Château-d'Oex; then go via Rougemont to Saanen and pick up the main tour again at the 116km-point — via Gstaad, Col du Pillon and Col de la Croix back to Aigle. 100km; 2h30min driving.

(3) Gruyère region (central Fribourg) and Vaud highlands (Pays d'Enhaut) only: instead of starting in Aigle, pick up the main tour at the 33km-point and do the loop Château-d'Oex, Gruyères, Jaun Pass, Zweisimmen, Saanen, Rougemont, Château-d'Oex. 87km; 2h15min driving.

The starting point, **Aigle**, can be reached from the A9 motorway, exit 17 (AIGLE). Follow signs to AIGLE CENTRE. Immediately after crossing the bridge over the river **Grande Eau**, fork right and stop at one of the car parks. Aigle is wine country and features a many-turreted castle amidst vineyards (◼M; www.chateauaigle.ch).

Short walk: Aigle, its castle and the Circuit de Plantour (2km, 25min, negligible ascent, or 5km, 1h25min, ascent 200m). From the parking area enter the old village along its pedestrianised main street, the RUE DE BOURG. After 300m, turn left on

RUE DE LA GARE. Following the signs CHATEAU, you reach the CASTLE in 10 minutes. The castle is home to the Vine, Wine and Wine Label Museum (Musée de la vigne, du vin et de l'étiquette; **M** open Apr-Jun, Sep/Oct, Tue-Sun 11.00-18.00; Jul/Aug daily 11.00-18.00). From here you could just return to Aigle, but why not extend this stroll with the *Circuit de Plantour* — a signposted walk circling the tree-covered hill called **Plantour** by the castle? From the castle, continue on the surfaced road for about 350m, then turn right. Proceed for a good 100m and turn right again. Descend 100m, then leave the surfaced road, bearing left to take a woodland trail. Now you start to climb, and the ascent is quite steep. Ignore any side-trails and follow the yellow rhombus waymarks.

Some 20 minutes after you have entered the woods there is a five-sided wooden lookout, but the vegetation is quite high. The trail then makes a sharp bend, and you leave the forest five minutes later, now descending. After the route becomes a surfaced road, bear left, cross the railway line, and bear left again at the next junction. When you reach the castle, retrace your steps to Aigle. But in Aigle, instead of taking the Rue de Bourg back to the parking area, take the parallel RUE DE JERUSALEM just a few metres before Rue de Bourg — to admire the upper floors of the houses bridging the street.

Leave Aigle (0km) and follow the sign LES MOSSES. The winding road climbs past occasional lay-bys, some with view (📷), some without. At 10.5km ignore the junction for Leysin, a resort village; keep straight on. Just 1.5km further on, continue round the hairpin bend (12km). *(But for shorter tour 1, turn right here.)* **Les Mosses** (18km) is a small elongated skiing resort stretching up to the **Col des Mosses** (1445m). The road now enters the **Pays d'Enhaut** (21km) and goes through **L'Etivaz** (26km). The eponymous cheese is a hard cheese produced in about a hundred dairies in the Vaud Alps; the Maison de l'Etivaz (www.etivaz-aoc.ch) on the left-hand side of the road in the village features a slide show (in English), arranges visits to cheese cellars and has regional products for sale. Beyond the narrow **Gorges du Pissot** (30km), the valley widens up and you arrive in

Balloon festival in Château-d'Oex

Château-d'Oex (33km). The town is famous for its balloon festival in January. Instead of immediately turning left at the roundabout (towards Bulle), drive into the town and stop at the parking area about 200m from the roundabout.

Short walk: Château-d'Oex
(1km, 30min, 60m ascent). From the parking area walk up the main street, LE PETIT PRÉ. Climb up to the CHURCH on the prominent hill guarding the town (photograph on pages 30-31). On one side of the hill there is a beautiful flower garden, **Jardin de la Motte**. There are benches in this garden and around the church, offering superb spots for a picnic.

From Château-d'Oex I highly recommend a 14km return detour east to lovely **Rougemont** (*not included in the overall km readings*), where you can see some adorable chalets. Notice, too, just before the roundabout at the entrance to the village, the church and castle on the right.

Short walk: Rougemont
(1km-4km, 20min-1h30min, ascent 30m-200m). Park at the car park near the railway station. Walk up the main village road and admire the wooden chalets with carvings and inscriptions. At the HOTEL DE COMMUNE, bear left and, immediately afterwards, left again. This takes you to the TOURIST OFFICE, where the short version of this walk turns back. But if you're ready for something slightly more strenuous, continue along the road towards SAANEN at the junction just past the tourist office. At the bridge (**Pont de Combabelle**), leave the surfaced road and bear left on a path signposted to CHATEAU-D'OEX. The path climbs (sometimes steeply), then flattens out 15 minutes above the bridge. You cross mountain pastures and after another 20 minutes reach a road which you follow back to **Rougemont** (signposted).

From the roundabout in Château-d'Oex (33km; *47km if you took the detour to Rougemont*) follow the sign BULLE.

The short walk around the lake near Montbovon at first runs past this fine viewpoint over the village; there's a well-placed picnic table nearby.

View south from above the Col de la Croix, to the Dents du Midi

The village of **Rossinière**
(37km) makes for another very
worthwhile stop. Turn right
300m after the village sign and
follow the parking signs to the
parking area about 200m
higher up, near the church.

**Short walk: Le Grand Chalet
and a circuit around Lake
Vernex** (4km, 1h, ascent 100m).
Even if you don't take this short
walk, *do* picnic on the bench
under the tree by the church
shown on page 29 — with a view
of the village, the lake and the
surrounding mountains. Life
doesn't get much better than
this. For the walk, go down to
the main road through
Rossinière and turn left. After
about 150m turn right and
descend 100m. At the corner is
Le Grand Chalet, one of the
largest and most beautiful
wooden buildings in the canton.
The house has 113 windows and
is decorated with carvings,
paintings and inscriptions. It was
owned by the painter Balthus
who lived in Rossinière and died
there in 2001; his grave can be
visited at the chapel. Continue to
the RAILWAY STATION, cross the

railway line, pass the CEMETERY,
cross the river and walk up the
gently sloping road. Turn right
at the junction 200m beyond the
bridge. Past a couple of farms,
you soon see **Lake Vernex**. At
the western end of the lake, cross
the small dam and follow the
road beside the lake back to
Rossinière.

After Rossinière, the next stop
is **Montbovon** (44km).

**Short walk: around the lake
near Montbovon** (3.8km,
1h20min, ascent 110m). About
1.3km after the village centre of
Montbovon, turn sharp right
following signs to the parking
area alongside the small road.
Walk the few metres to the
railway crossing and continue
straight ahead on the gravel path
(signpost: TOUR DU LAC PAR LE
COMMIN). After 50m you pass a
picnic table and cross a BRIDGE
(actually four adjoining bridges).
Turn right, go under the bridge
and rise up again on the far side.
Walk on the roadside bank and
into the woods. The path climbs
quite steeply, but only for a short
time. Then you descend through

Boardwalks in the Gorges de la Jogne (left) and the dam at Lake Montsalvens, where the walk through the Gorges de la Jogne ends, before you return the same way.
Bottom: Walk 15 begins here at Lac Retaud, but you can just take a short stroll from the nearby car park and restaurant.

pastures to **Montbovon**. Follow the through road for 150m, then cross the railway, turn left and go downhill. Over the bridge, pass the small *POWER PLANT* and follow the track across pastures. At a junction, the trail makes a U-turn and descends. You cross an old *COVERED WOODEN BRIDGE* dating from the 17th century and return to the parking place. There are pleasant picnic spots by the lake, not far from the parking area.

From Montbovon continue on the road past various villages, to arrive in **Epagny** (57km). At the roundabout here, take the turn-off for *GRUYERES*. In Pringy, just before crossing the railway line, the road makes a U-turn and heads up to **Gruyères**. Gruyères is an extremely picturesque medieval castle village (see photograph on pages 118-119) — and a very popular tourist attraction, so you may have to park some

way distant. Cars are banned in the village's only street. There are several parking areas in succession at the foot of the hill, each closer to the village.

Short walk: **Stroll through Gruyères** (1h to half a day, depending on visits). The castle can be visited (**Château de Gruyères** ∎ open Apr-Oct 9.00-18.00, Nov-Mar 10.00-16.30, www.chateau-gruyeres.ch). The famous cheese is named after the *region* Gruyère (without the 's'). There is a dairy in **Pringy**, where you can watch cheese being made — the **Maison du Gruyère** (open Jun-Sep 9.00-19.00, Oct-May 9.00-18.00, www.lamaisondugruyere.ch). It is just opposite Pringy's *RAILWAY STATION* — about a 15-minute walk from Gruyères (a descent/re-ascent of 70m). Cheese is made only three or four times a day, so if you want to see the process, be sure to visit between 9.00-11.00 or 12.30-14.30.

Drive back from Gruyères to the roundabout in **Epagny** (61km) and turn left. After 150m turn right for *JAUNPASS*. Go through the town of **Broc** and, a few hundred metres further on (just before the bridge over the river Jogne), follow the parking sign for the **Gorges de la Jogne**. The car park is 200m from the main road, in the forest (⩗).

Short walk: **Gorges de la Jogne** (4.5km, 1h15min, ascent around 150m). Walk ahead on the wide gravel road for less than 10 minutes, then enter the gorge through a *TUNNEL*. This narrow gorge with its bridges, boardwalks, steps and tunnels — to the accompaniment of

murmuring water — makes for a very pleasant and relaxing walk after busy Gruyères. At first the trail runs beside the **Jogne** stream, then rises 30m-50m above it, before it descends again, crosses the stream once more and — after a steep finish — reaches **Lake Montsalvens** with its dam (⌂). Walk back the same way.

Back on the road, continue towards the Jaunpass via the towns of **Charmey** (70km) and **Jaun** (80km). When you're driving through Jaun, watch out on the right for the small but impressive **waterfall** (you can stop in the village and walk to the waterfall in a few minutes).
Then climb the **Jaunpass** (1509m, 88km). After the pass, the view widens up over the **Simmen Valley** (Simmen-

tal; about 1km down from the pass there's a lay-by with an orientation table (📷). The descent is winding all the way down to canton route 11. Turn right here (96km) and come into **Zweisimmen** (103km). From Zweisimmen you could take a 35km return detour *(not included in the km readings)* into the Simmental. Lenk is its main village; drive 4.5km beyond Lenk to Oberried and then to the very head of the valley to admire the Simmen Falls and perhaps take the short walk below.

Short walk: Simmen Falls
(1.7km, 45min, ascent 140m). Park at the HOTEL SIMMENFÄLLE at the end of the road (1102m; ⛰). It's just a two-minute walk to the lower viewpoint, from where you can see the steeply falling **Simme** stream

The foothills of Les Diablerets, from above the Col de la Croix

pleasant shopping street through the village, there is not much to see. Continue to **Gsteig** (130km) and start the climb to the **Col du Pillon** (1546m, 137km; 🚡) with Les Diablerets, the highest mountain in the Vaud Alps, as its magical backdrop. The pass is also the departure point of a cable car to the year-round Glacier 3000 skiing area.

Short walk: Lac Retaud (500m, 15min, ascent negligible). Some 100m after the sign at the **Col du Pillon**, a narrow road winds upward to **Lac Retaud** (1.8km; large car park; 🍴). Take a stroll around the lake, relax in the grass and have a swim in the summer. You can also start Walk 15 from here.

From the pass descend to the village of **Les Diablerets** (140km) and, 1.2km after the town sign, turn left to climb to the **Col de la Croix** (1778m, 150km; snow-free May-Nov). On the way down, you pass through the villages of **Villars-sur-Ollon** (157km) and **Ollon** (167km) before arriving back in **Aigle** (174km).

plummeting down some 700m like a waterfall. Climb the trail just beside the Simme; a sign (in German) says that this trail should only be used *to ascend*. When you reach a bridge (**Barbarabrücke**, 1240m) you will see the STREAM spitting out of the rock. The amount of water is highest after thunderstorms or when snow and glaciers melt. For the descent, take the unmade road (benches).

From Zweisimmen (103km *excluding the detour*), continue on route 11 to **Saanen** (116km), then branch off left to **Gstaad** (119km). Gstaad is one of the most chichi and exclusive mountain resorts in the world, playing host to major events like an international tennis tournament and the Yehudi Menuhin Music Festival. But except for the

Car tour 6 (Bernese Oberland): LAKE THUN AND LAKE BRIENZ, GRINDELWALD AND LAUTERBRUNNEN

Thun • Beatus Caves • Unterseen • Interlaken • Brienz • Ballenberg with Swiss Open-Air Museum • Aare Gorge • Reichenbach Falls • Iseltwald and Giessbach Falls • Lauterbrunnen • Grindelwald • Spiez • Thun

177km/110mi; 3h driving
En route: Walks 16-20; additional short walks suggested below

---

This circuit navigates around two splendid lakes in the Bernese Oberland, Lake Thun (Thunersee) and Lake Brienz (Brienzersee) and features side-trips into the Hasli and Lauterbrunnen valleys — and the valley which is home to Grindelwald.

From **Thun** follow the northern shore of **Lake Thun** towards GUNTEN and INTER-LAKEN, with open views across the lake and pyramid-shaped Mount Niesen rising behind Spiez on the southern shore. Pass through Hilterfingen, Oberhofen, **Gunten** and **Merligen** to arrive at **Beaten-bucht** (14km).
From here you could follow part of the 'Pilgerweg' as a short walk to the Beatus Caves (see below), but if you prefer to drive there, just continue the tour to the 17km-point.
Yet another option is to take a funicular up to Beatenberg (1121m) and from there a gondola up Mount Niederhorn (1934m), enjoy the view and walk down to Beatenbucht in about 2h30min.

Short walk: Pilgrim's path from Beatenbucht to the Beatus Caves

(3.5km, 1h, ascent 230m). Park in the multi-storey car park in **Beatenbucht**. Walk to the adjacent valley station of the funicular and follow the yellow signs towards BEATENBUCHT/ PILGERWEG. The pilgrims' path is part of the Camino de Santiago (the Way of St James) and runs through forest high above Lake

Thun from Beatenbucht to the **Beatus Caves** (description below, photograph opposite), with occasional views over the lake. From the caves descend for 10min to the road and take the bus back to Beatenbucht (runs every 30min-1h; timetable at the caves).

From Beatenbucht, the road starts to rise, reaching 70m above the lake by the time you reach the **Beatus Caves** (17km ∩✸⋒M open mid-Mar to mid-Oct, 30min guided tours, www.beatushoehlen.ch). These 1km-long illuminated drip-stone caves are set up in the cliffs amidst waterfalls. From the caves the road drops again as you approach the plain with the towns Unterseen and its larger neighbour, adjacent Interlaken, sandwiched in between the two lakes. At the eastern end of Lake Thun, follow the sign for UNTERSEEN (*not* Interlaken). In **Unterseen** (22km), follow the TRANSIT signs, to avoid the centre of **Interlaken**; then follow the *blue* sign for LUCERNE. (The green sign to Lucerne would take you to the expressway on the southern shore of Lake Brienz, but we want to cruise the northern shore first.)

On the northern shore there are a number of lay-bys () which invite you to stop and enjoy the scenery as you pass through the villages of **Ringgenberg**, **Niederried** and **Oberried** to arrive in **Brienz** (43km), an attractive lakeside resort known for its wood carvings. It is also the starting point of the mountain railway which climbs Mount Rothorn (2350m; follow signs for parking at the eastern end of Brienz).

About 2km after Brienz, after you have left the village Brienz-Kienholz, take a left towards *FREILICHTMUSEUM BALLENBERG*. After 2km you come to the

Bridge over waterfalls at the Beatus Caves

western entrance to **Ballenberg** — home of the outstanding **Swiss Open-Air Museum** (M✕ open mid-Apr to end Oct, ℂ 033 952 10 30 or 033 952 10 40. www.ballenberg.ch). Over a hundred historical buildings threatened with destruction (some of them centuries old) were dismantled and re-erected in Ballenberg. They come from all over Switzerland, and are set in appropriate gardens or fields. The authentic interiors of the rooms give an impression of life's hardships in years gone by. All species of native Swiss farm animals are on view (there are over 250 different animals), and there are demonstrations of typical crafts. Children love it.

Short walk: Open-Air Museum in Ballenberg (time immaterial). You can spend from an hour to a full day in this park. Pick up the LEAFLET at the entrance (which is also served by bus from the railway station in Brienz). The leaflet describes two 2h walks from the west entrance; there are also two recommended 2h walks from the east entrance. Or you can take the 4h walk across the entire area. Naturally you can also just ramble at will through the park.

From Ballenberg head back to the main road (49km) and turn left towards MEIRINGEN. Now you come into the **Haslital**, a large valley stretching from Lake Brienz to the Grimsel Pass. The road parallels the river **Aare**. At the roundabout where a left turn would cross the Aare and enter Meiringen, continue *straight on*. Then go right at the next roundabout (69km), signposted to the

GRIMSELPASS. After 100m you come to a crossroads. First take the road to the left; in just over 1km you come to the western entrance to the **Aare Gorge** (entrance open Apr-Oct from 9.00-17.00, but from 8.00-18.00 in Jul/Aug; you can exit any time; in Jul/Aug also open Wed and Fri from 21.00-23.00 when the gorge is floodlit, www.aareschlucht.ch).

Short walk: Aare Gorge (3km, 1h30min, ascent 50m or 30-40min if returning by public transport; see below). The **Aare River** has carved an impressive gorge 1.4km long and up to 180m deep — with its walls only a metre across at the narrowest point. The gorge has been made accessible to walkers through a bold system: there's 1km of wooden paths built on steel girders anchored in the cliff walls, punctuated by some 400m of tunnels. The walk is easy with little ascent — but spectacular. This is a linear walk — out and back the same way. Using public transport, you can visit the gorge on a one-way walk (about 30-40min). There are two entrances to the gorge, west (ℂ 033 971 40 48) and east (ℂ 033 971 10 48), both of which can be reached by the Meiringen-Innertkirchen Bahn, which usually runs every 30min. It's a 10min walk to the west entrance, a 5min walk to the east entrance (crossing the swingbridge that you see at the eastern end of the gorge).

Drive back to the crossroads, and now go straight ahead, after 300m coming to the valley station of the funicular for the **Reichenbach Falls** (runs mid-May until beginning Oct, 9.00-11.45 and 13.15-17.45 every 15min; Jul/Aug

9.00-18.00 every 15min; photograph on page 61).

Short walk: Reichenbach Falls and Sherlock Holmes (3km, 1h30min, ascent 140m, descent 380m).

Of the many waterfalls in the Bernese Oberland, the Reichenbach Falls impressed Sir Arthur Conan Doyle so much that he let his fictional detective Sherlock Holmes 'die' here — the exact place is marked by a star on the cliff wall, clearly visible from the mountain station of the funicular. From the funicular MOUNTAIN STATION (843m), follow the waymarked path to the falls. You cross the impressive **Reichenbach Falls** via a BRIDGE and come in about 25 minutes to GASTHAUS ZWIRGI (980m, 🏠🍴✆ 033 971 14 22, www.zwirgi. ch). You have two choices to return on foot to the valley. You can retrace your steps a few metres and then take the path signposted east via **Schwendi** (at the first junction in the forest, turn left to get to the Sherlock Holmes memorial); this takes about an hour. Alternatively, take the path west from Gasthaus Zwirgi via **Falcheren** (allow 1h30min).

After these two visits, return to the main road (72km) and drive back to Lake Brienz. Follow the *green* signs for INTERLAKEN which will take you to the southern shore of Lake Brienz (do *not* follow the blue sign to Interlaken, as this route leads to the northern shore). The expressway runs some way distant from the lake and goes through several tunnels, but still offers glimpses of the lake. Leave the expressway to drive down to the small and quiet village of **Iseltwald** on the

At the narrowest point, the walls of the Aare Gorge are only 1m apart

shore of **Lake Brienz** (92km; closed to traffic, except for guests of the hotels and restaurants). There are a few hotels, an open-air swimming pool and the pier for boats plying the lake. The car park is outside the village.

Short walk: Iseltwald and the Giessbach Falls (as far as you like — or, as a circuit via the Grandhotel Giessbach, up to 12km, 3h30min, ascent of about 200m).

The walk from **Iseltwald** to the Giessbach Falls is gorgeous and just beside the lake — often in forest, with beautiful vistas. Only the sound of rippling water accompanies you. At various places the path has been dynamited into the rocks. You can go as far as you like and return the same way. If you'd like to set a moderate goal, you could just walk to the picnic area with fire places called **Glooten**, in the forest about half way between Iseltwald and the falls; this takes about 1h out and back. If you go all the way to **Giessbach** (about 1h30min), you'll find just a funicular by the pier — the oldest funicular in Europe, so the sign says. It goes up to the *GRANDHOTEL GIESSBACH*. You could take that up to save the climb, or you could walk up. To walk up, continue past the *PIER* and along the lake for a few metres, passing the lowest of the 14 cascades making up the **Giessbach Falls**, then take the signposted path up to the hotel. The best view of the falls is from the hotel. Now you can either go back the same way along the shoreline, or make a circuit by taking a path which runs about 150m above Lake Brienz. For the latter, continue uphill from the hotel for a few minutes, cross the falls again, and head back to Iseltwald on the broad gravel road — mostly through forest and some pastures. Near the end the road becomes surfaced. There are a handful of junctions where you can descend to the trail on the shore, if you decide to do so.

Drive back to the expressway and, south of Interlaken, take the exit signposted to *GRINDELWALD* for side-trips into the Lauterbrunnen Valley and Grindelwald. When you come to the hamlet of **Zwei-lütschinen** (109km), the road forks. Continue straight on through the village of **Lauter-brunnen** and leave your car at the signposted parking area by the church (114km). The **Lauterbrunnen Valley** is a miniature 'Yosemite of the Alps'. Dozens of waterfalls thunder down here. The two most famous are the **Staub-bach Falls** (Switzerland's highest freefalling waterfall, plummeting almost 300m — just a couple of minutes outside Lauterbrunnen and visible from the village) and the spectacular **Trümmelbach**

Falls. The latter are Europe's only glacial falls inside a mountain, draining the glaciers of the Eiger, Mönch and Jung-frau. A lift, tunnels, bridges and walkways bring the visitor close to these thundering falls.

Short walk: from Lauter-brunnen to the Staubbach Falls and Trümmelbach Falls (5min the Staubbach Falls; 3km/45min to the Trümmelbach Falls, return the same way or take the post bus which runs every 30min-1h; ascent negligible). From the *CHURCH*, follow the surfaced road to the **Staubbach Falls**, and continue along the path in the valley to the **Trümmelbach Falls**. Allow 30min for a visit to the Trümmelbach Falls (fee).

From Lauterbrunnen return to Zweilütschinen where you can branch off right to **Grindel-wald** (130km). If you plan to spend some time around Grin-delwald, Walk 19 (page 137) is short and spectacular. Do plan to stay a few days to enjoy one of the great landscapes of Switzerland, explored in detail in Walks 16-19.

From Grindelwald drive back to the Zweilütschinen junction (142km) and return to the expressway. Continue along the southern shore of Lake Thun, then take the exit for *SPIEZ*. Shortly after entering **Spiez**, there is a lay-by (☎) with a beautiful view to what Spiez claims is 'Europe's most beautiful bay' and its prom-inent castle. And beautiful the bay certainly is, embedded between hills and vineyards and with the pyramid-shaped Mount Niesen (2362m) towering up in the south. Descend to the bay at the shore of **Lake Thun** (167km; car park), where I suggest two short walks.

Short walk: Spiez and its vineyards (3km, 1h, ascent 100m).
From the garden of the CASTLE (▪ open Mar-Oct, ☎ 033 654 15 06, www.schloss-spiez.ch), follow the road to the Kirschgarten junction and turn right towards SPIEZBERG. Stroll around the vineyards and the forest of Spiezberg at your leisure, then return to the castle.

Short walk: Lakeside walk from Spiez to Faulensee and back
(6km, 1h30min, no height gain). From the bay, follow the path alongside the lake to the port of **Faulensee**. Trees bending over to touch the water, an open-air art museum, and a fish farm with information boards add to the charm of this peaceful walk.

From here head back to **Thun** (177km), where another lakeside walk is recommended.

Short walk: Lakeside walk from Thun to Gwatt (3km, 45min, no height gain). From STRANDBAD, the huge public indoor and outdoor swimming pool in the urban area of **Dürrenast**) follow the signposted and waymarked lakeside walk to the village of Gwatt. The first few minutes lead through sports and residential areas, then the path runs by reeds at the water's edge. In **Gwatt**, walk to the main street and take the bus back to Strandbad.

On the short walk to the Reichenbach Falls, just a few metres from Gasthaus Zwirgi, there is a fine view over Meiringen.

Car tour 7 (Valais): WINE ROUTE FROM MARTIGNY TO LEUK

Martigny • Fully • Saillon • Leytron • Chamoson • Vétroz • Sion • St-Léonard • Sierre • Salgesch • Varen • Leuk

53km/33mi one way; 1h15min driving
En route: Walk 21; additional short walks suggested below

There are three different 'wine routes' (*chemin du vignoble* in French; *Weinweg* in German) in the Valais — one for hikers (66km), one for cyclists (83km) and one for motorised traffic (53km). All are described in great detail in a bilingual booklet (French/German, 124 pages) which can also be bought online at www. cheminduvignoble.ch or www.weinweg.ch.

The drive itself only takes a bit more than an hour, but you can easily fill one or two days by stopping at the places listed below, wining and dining and taking some of the short walks. You may also wish to combine the drive with sections of Walk 21 which covers the entire 66km distance on foot. The valley of Valais is broad, flat, and a true fruit basket, with many orchards and vineyards. In addition to the A9 motorway which goes up the valley as far as Sierre there is the main cantonal route 9 and some secondary roads. The 'wine route' is a combination of secondary roads and cantonal route 9 and is labeled by the stylized emblem of the Valais in the form of a bunch of grapes.

Take exit 21, MARTIGNY/FULLY, off the A9 motorway, and make for FULLY. Cross the **Rhône River** (1km) and continue to **Fully** (2km).

Short walk — Chestnut forest (1km, 30min, ascent 50m). Fully boasts a very large chestnut forest (15ha) — the first trees having been planted around 1200. Chestnuts were a staple food for the poor, and each family owned a few trees which helped them to survive. A NATURE TRAIL with 14 information boards leads through the forest (*not* to be confused with the jogging path called *Vitaparcours* which also runs through here). Signs featuring a SMILING CHESTNUT show you the

way. To reach the starting point of the trail, take a left turn shortly after the centre of Fully (signed CHATAIGNERAIE). The road rises fairly steeply for 300m, with several parking areas at the side. You are allowed to collect chestnuts found on the ground for your own consumption (but they only fall in October).

Heading east from Fully, a medieval tower, Saillon's landmark is visible from afar. **Saillon** (9km) is definitely worth exploring, with its picturesque old village sitting on a jutting hill amidst vineyards. Saillon markets itself around the legendary Farinet, a sort of Robin Hood of the Alps, who made and distributed counterfeit coins to the poor in the 1870s and who tried to find refuge in Saillon — but died here under mysterious circumstances at the age of 35. Among other things, Farinet's name is used to denote a walk (*Sentier à Farinet*, also called *Sentier aux Vitraux*) — a path adorned by 21 sculptures made from stained glass windows, a museum of counterfeit money (*Musée de la fausse monnaie*) and the world's smallest registered vineyard — just 1.618m^2!

Tour continues on page 48

Descending from the village of Chamoson, you come into the largest wine-growing area in the Valais.

WATER TOWER OF EUROPE

Water and ice play a central role in Switzerland. Hydrologically speaking, the country is the water tower of Europe: rivers flow in all four directions and empty into four different oceans. Supposedly you are never more than 20km from a lake in Switzerland. The Valais in particular offers some of the most mind-boggling structures erected by mankind to make use of water.

Bisse/Suone

With one of the lowest rainfall rates in Switzerland, it has always been a challenge in the Valais to bring water to the vineyards and fields. So water irrigation channels, called *bisse* in the french-speaking part of Switzerland and *Suone* in the German-speaking part of the Valais, were built — some dating back as far as the 13th century. Some of these water conduits still carry water today, and there are often walking paths beside them. This guide describes walks alongside the following irrigation channels:
• Car tour 7 has a stroll along the modest **Bisse du Poteu** in Grugnay.
• The Valais vineyard trail (Walk 21) features the very beautiful **Bisse de Clavoz** from Sion and the **Varen Suone** (near Leuk).
• Walk 24 follows the **Bisse de Chervé**, although hardly any signs remain of it today.

Bisse de Clavoz (Walk 21)

• Walk 26 explores the **Bisse du Ro** — the most vertiginous and spectacular Bisse in the Valais.

What a contrast between those daring water irrigation channels and the other incredible engineering feat, the hydroelectric dams.

Dams

The **Grande Dixence Dam** is the largest so-called heavy dam in the world — a wall 285m high, 700m long, 200m thick at the base, 15m at the top and weighing 15 million tons. With the amount of concrete used to build the dam, a wall 1.5m high and 10cm wide could be built around the earth. The 32km of tunnels and inspection shafts inside this concrete monster allow staff to constantly monitor the dam. After the first Dixence Dam was built (1930-1935, with a storage capacity of 50 million cublic metres), the Grande Dixence was constructed from 1951 to 1965.

The dam holds back the **Lac des Dix**, a lake more than 5km long. When the lake is full by the end of September, it is up to 284m deep and contains 400 million cublic metres of water. In April, the lake is at its lowest level. Two-thirds of the catchment area is covered by some 50 glaciers. Inside the surrounding mountains are

Aletsch Glacier, Walk 32, and the Grande Dixence Dam, Walk 25

100km of tunnels, including a 24km-long main water conduit in the heart of the mountains at 2400m altitude, which collect the waters flowing between Mischabel and Mont Gelé. Some 60% of the water that fills the Grande Dixence is actually pumped up from an altitude lower than the lake. Gravity only accounts for about 40% of the water flowing into the lake.

Arguably even more impressive, although smaller, is the **Mauvoisin Dam**, one of the world's highest arch dams and the second highest dam in Switzerland after the Grande Dixence. Completed in 1957 and heightened in 1991, the dam is today 250m high and the crest 520m long. The dam holds back the **Lac de Mauvoisin**, which, when full, contains about half as much water as the Lac des Dix. There are four walks to dams and their lakes in this guide:

• The short walk in the Gorges de la Jogne (Car tour 5) leads to the **Montsalvens Dam**, shown on p34.

• Walk 23 returns via the wall of the **Mauvoisin Dam**.

• Walk 24 explores **Cleuson** (constructed 1947-1951), with a capacity of 20 million cubic metres.

• Walk 25 visits the **Grande Dixence**.

Glaciers

None of the walks in this guide crosses a glacier (you should do this only with a qualified guide), but several get pretty close! One of the most spectacular hikes is Walk 32 along the **Aletsch Glacier**. There are also good views of glaciers in Walks 18, 19 and 27-31.

Short walk: Sentier à Farinet

(3km, 1h, ascent 110m). This short walk can easily be extended to 3-4h if you admire all the places of interest dotted along the path and have an *al fresco lunch* at one of the restaurants. After having driven past the Saillon village sign, the road makes a 90° turn to the left and, shortly thereafter, one to the right. Leave your car 600m further on, in a car park on your left (sign: BOURG), which is the starting point of the walk (there is another car park uphill on the right, next to the old village up on the hill). Walk back along the roadside pavement, passing the first six works of art. At the one called *Silence,* take the path to the right. After a short but sharp climb, you enter the **old village of Saillon** through a gate. Some 50m from the gate you'll find the **Musée de la Fausse Monnaie** (M open Apr-Oct, Wed-Sun, 14.00-17.00; Nov-Mar, Fri-Sun, same hours). The MEDIEVAL GARDEN surrounding the church here in old Saillon is a gem. What did people in the Valais eat between the 10th and 15th centuries, before tomatoes, peppers, pumpkins, zucchini, potatoes, corn or green beans found their way from America to Europe? This garden exhibits some 500 species, excellently labelled, that were used in medieval Valais as vegetables or medication. Leave the old village through another gate, marvel at the traditional tools on display close to the sculpture *Plaisir,* and make your way up to the ruins of Saillon's MEDIEVAL CASTLE (■). Climb up the tower and enjoy a view across the entire Rhône Valley. Then retrace your steps to the display of traditional tools and continue uphill on the road. When you reach the sculpture *Destin,* take the road forking left. At the next sculpture, *Mort,* leave the road and continue on the gravel path for 100m. You now enter an ALLEY OF IMMORTALITY, where the wisdom of the famous (and non-famous) is inscribed on plates. At the top of the mound is the WORLD'S SMALLEST VINE-YARD — only three vines. Today it belongs to the Dalaï Lama.

From Saillon continue the drive through **Leytron** to **Chamoson** (14km) which, with over 400ha, boasts the largest wine-growing area in Valais. Before continuing on the wine route towards Sion, you may like to consider visiting two other villages (*not* included in the overall km readings).

The first is **Grugnay**, a hamlet 1.5km above Chamoson (signposted at the exit from Chamoson). In Grugnay, follow signs and park at the small **Musée de Spéléologie** (Museum of Potholing; M open year round Tue-Sun, 9.00-12.00 and 14.00-17.30; www.museespeleo.ch). From this museum, you can walk alongside the irrigation channel **Bisse du Poteu** (see page 46), which carries water starting in May.

The second village is **St-Pierre-de-Clages** (⚲), about 1.5km from Chamoson towards the valley (also signposted). In addition to its Romanesque church with octagonal tower, St-Pierre-de-Clages is also famous for its bookshops (it's called 'Le Village Suisse du Livre') and its book festival (Fête du Livre) which takes place during the last weekend in August. You can easily lose track of time browsing through all the second-hand books on display in various shops.

Otherwise, continue on the road you have been following from Chamoson straight towards ARDON. Joining main route 9, turn left into **Ardon**. Then pass through **Magnot** and adjacent **Vétroz** (20km).

Short walk: Promenade de l'Amigne (2.7km, 45min, ascent about 150m, all on surfaced road). **Vétroz** also has its vineyard trail, the *Promenade de l'Amigne* through vineyards (map and description of highlights en route at www.amigne.ch/en/ acceuil. html). Branch off left from the main road, when you see a parking sign. The walk starts at the PLACE DU FOUR (Oven Square), a small semi-circular open-air theatre some 100m from the church. Opposite the church is the RELAIS DU VALAIS, an imposing former abbey which today hosts two restaurants and an oenothèque with a large collection of regional wines. When facing the *relais,* take the path to the right which leads you up into the VINEYARDS. The walk is waymarked.

After Vétroz, follow signs for SION. Just before entering Sion you pass one of the hills jutting up near the town, **Mont d'Orge** (or 'Montorge'). French-speaking **Sion** (26km, ▉✝M, pop 27,000 — but double that during the day) is the capital of Valais. It tried very hard to host the Olympic Games in 2002 and 2006 — with the world-famous ski resorts of Verbier, Crans-Montana and Zermatt nearby — but failed. Sion has a beautiful medieval centre with a maze of cobbled alleys, and all the points of interest (museums, churches, historic houses) can easily be visited on foot. Two landmarks visible from afar are Tourbillon Castle (north) and Valère Castle (south), each atop its eponymous hillock.

Short walk: Mont d'Orge (4km-7.5km, 1h30min-2h30min, ascent 300m). From the RAILWAY STATION in Sion, walk up busy Avenue de la Gare to Rue de Lausanne and turn left (to the right is Place de la Planta with the tourist office). At Rue des

From the short walk up Mont d'Orge there is a fine view over Sion, with the castles of Tourbillon (left, in ruins) and Valère (right) rising above the Rhône.

Amandiers, turn right. Cross Avenue du Petit-Chasseur and continue on Chemin des Amandiers for 200m, then turn right and, after 100m, join Chemin des Lézards. Just above the HOSPITAL, follow Rue de Gravelone, rising through vineyards. After 300m, bear right on Chemin du Lac-de-Montorge. From the Lac de Mont d'Orge PARKING AREA (50min from the railway station; 643m), it's 20min up to the summit of **Mont d'Orge** (786m). A road to the left, then a path, climbs left to CASTLE RUINS, with splendid view over Sion and the Rhône Valley. Return to the parking area and stroll round the reed-fringed **Lac de Mont d'Orge** (1km, 15min). Then either return the same way, or walk up 200m to the main road, for a bus back to Sion.

From Sion, follow signs for BRIG. The wine route runs beside the **Rhône** for a fairly long stretch. In **Uvrier** (31km) you could treat yourself to an overnight stay at the Hotel des Vignes (🛏 ☎ 027 203 16 71, www.hoteldesvignes.ch) and dine at the distinguished restaurant Au Cep de Vigne (☎ 027 203 53 00, www.aucepdevigne.ch). Adjacent **St-Léonard** (32km) boasts Europe's largest underground lake — 300m long, 20m wide, 10m deep (open mid-Mar to Oct, ☎ 027 203 22 66, www.st-leonard.ch or www.lac-souterrain.com). To get there, follow the LAC SOUTERRAIN signs; the car park is 300m off the main road. There's a 20-30min boat ride across the lake on offer.

Continue to **Sierre** (42km, pop 14,000), where French is the preferred language.

VINEA, Switzerland's largest wine fair (www.vinea.ch), takes place here every year during the first weekend in September. Sierre is home to the Valaisian Museum of Wine and Winegrowing *(French: Musée Valaisan de la Vigne et du Vin; German: Walliser Reb- und Weinmuseum);* it's housed in the Château de Villa northwest of the centre, at the end of Avenue du Marché (M open Apr-Nov, Tue-Fri, 14.00-17.00, also throughout the year on request for groups of 10 or more, ☎ 027 456 35 25, www. museevalaisanduvin.ch). There is a second part to the museum which is in the neighbouring German-speaking village of Salgesch. To reach Salgesch from Sierre, follow signs to BRIG, then SALGESCH. The parking area in **Salgesch** (46km) is next to the church; follow signs to the museum, a walk of about 300m (M same opening hours as above, ☎ 027 456 45 25, www.sierre-salgesch.ch).

From Salgesch take the narrow road climbing to VAREN, the next village on the wine route. In **Varen** (50km) stop in the parking area next to the road and walk the few metres to the church (⛪☞) which sits somewhat hidden behind a mound on a rocky spur, with a great view up and down the Rhône Valley and across Switzerland's largest pine wood, Pfyn-Finges (www.pfyn-finges.ch). There is a path — also a bit hidden — to the top of the rock. It starts at the steps in front of the house before the church. The rock is a lovely picnic spot. The final destination on the wine route is **Leuk** (53km), a village with some beautiful ancient buildings.

Car tour 8: SIDE-VALLEYS OF THE VALAIS

**Side-valleys and passes south of the Rhône (from west to east):
Vallée du Trient • Val d'Entremont (Great St-Bernard Pass)
with Val Ferret • Val de Bagnes • Val de Nendaz • Val
d'Hérémence • Val d'Hérens with Val d'Arolla • Val d'Anniviers
with Val de Moiry and Val de Zinal • Mattertal • Saastal**

Times and distances shown below
En route: Walks 22-25, 27-30

**Side-valleys and passes north of the Rhône (from west to east):
Lac de Derborence • Sanetschsee • Lac de Tseuzier • Crans-
Montana • Leukerbad • Lötschental • Bettmeralp**

Times and distances shown below
En route: Walks 26, 31, 32

While the main valley traversed by the river Rhône is splendid in its own right (see Car tour 7), what really enthralls visitors to the Valais is the juxtaposition of towering mountains with impressive glaciers and lush pastures dotted with fragile huts — the landscapes on view in the tributary valleys.

The following description is not intended as a single 'car tour' (all those curves would make you dizzy), nor is it an exhaustive listing of all the Valais valleys. It is simply an appetizer, to whet your taste for exploring this marvelous part of Switzerland.

Martigny • Vallée du Trient • Lac d'Emosson

36km/22mi; 1h driving one way
The narrow Trient Valley leads from Martigny to the **Col de la Forclaz** (1526m). The main village is **Trient** (1279m) on the far side of the col. The last village on Swiss soil is Le Châtelard, before the road continues into Mont Blanc country (Chamonix) in France. Not far *before* Le Châtelard, a road to the right leads to the village of **Finhaut**, and from there a scenic road rises in sweeping serpentine bends to the **Lac d'Emosson** (parking at 1930m), with a magnificent view of Mont Blanc.

Martigny • Val d'Entremont • Great St-Bernard Pass

45km/28mi; 1h driving one way
En route: Walk 22
South of Martigny sees the start of St-Bernard country. Take exit 21 (MARTIGNY) off the A9 motorway. The road divides in **Sembrancher**, an attractive medieval village. The main road continues south to **Orsières** (820m). In Orsières, the valley divides into **Val Ferret**, one of the quieter valleys of Valais, and the main valley, **Val d'Entremont**. The main road passes through the villages of Liddes and **Bourg-St-Pierre** (1632m). Shortly after Bourg-St-Pierre the road enters the 5.9km-long Grand St-Bernard tunnel which emerges in Italy. Instead of going through the tunnel, take the narrow road off right which winds up to the **Great St-Bernard Pass** (2470m). There are around a dozen major north-south pass routes in the Swiss Alps, of which the Great St-Bernard Pass is the

One of the Lacs de Fenêtre (Walk 22, from the Great St-Bernard Pass)

oldest historically — crossed by both individuals and entire armies. The pass is snow-free from around June to October. The view from the pass is limited, but history and marvellous Walk 22 make the pass a tremendous goal.

Martigny • Val de Bagnes • Mauvoisin Dam

37km/23mi, 45min driving one way
En route: Walk 23

Take the road from Martigny to **Sembrancher**, then fork off left to **Le Châble** (from where a road zigzags up to the world-famous ski resort of Verbier). But instead take the road heading straight on from Le Châble into the quiet **Val de Bagnes**, going through the villages of Versegères, Champsec, Lourtier, **Fionnay** and Bonnatchiesse to the head of the valley (there are a couple of narrow tunnels en route, but lay-bys allow cars to pass). At the end of the road you come to the giant, 250m-high dam, the **Barrage de Mauvoisin** (see details on page 47, as well as the photograph on page 150 (Walk 23). From the base it's just a 15-minute walk to the top of the dam.

Sion • Val de Nendaz • Siviez • (Mont Fort)

Sion to Siviez: 17km/11mi; 30min driving one way
En route: Walk 24

From Sion, a wide road leads up to the ski resort of Haute-Nendaz. Shortly before arriving in the centre, fork off left into the **Val de Nendaz**. The road ends in **Siviez** (1733m), starting point for Walk 24 to the Lac de Cleuson (with another dam, but on a smaller scale than the one at Mauvoisin). Three chairlifts depart from Siviez, one of which goes to the Tortin station — from where you could take two cable cars in succession up to **Mont Fort** (3329m) with its fine views.

Sion • Val d'Hérémence • Barrage de la Grande Dixence

26km/17mi; 50min driving one way
En route: Walk 25

From **Sion** follow the signs first to the village of **Vex** and then **Hérémence**. Beyond Hérémence (after 18km), the road starts snaking upwards, until you arrive at the foot of the immense **Grande Dixence Dam** (26km; see details on page 46 and Walk 25 on page

153). On the way back turn right after 11km (37km in total) towards EUSEIGNE. In **Euseigne** you have two choices. Either make for SION and pass the **Pyramides d'Euseigne** (bizarre rock spikes in the valley 2km after Euseigne, with a dark boulder on top), or turn right into the **Val d'Hérens** (see below).

Sion • Val d'Hérens (with Val d'Arolla)

Sion to Arolla: 40km/25mi; 1h driving one way
From **Sion** follow the sign for VEX and in **Vex** continue to **Euseigne**, passing the **Pyramides d'Euseigne**. Continue to Evolène. Just after **Les Haudères**, you enter the **Val d'Arolla** with the village of **Arolla** (1998m) at its head.

Sierre • Val d'Anniviers (with Val de Moiry and Val de Zinal)

Sierre to Zinal: 30km/19mi; 45min driving one way
En route: Walk 27
From **Sierre** drive up the **Val d'Anniviers** to **Vissoie**. If you turn right in this village, you will reach **Grimentz**, one of the most beautiful villages in the Valais, from where you can drive to yet another dam at the **Lac de Moiry**. Alternatively, continue to **Zinal** (1675m), starting point for Walk 27.

Visp • Zermatt (Mattertal)

Visp to Täsch: 30km/19mi; 45min driving one way; then on to Zermatt by train
En route: Walks 28, 29
Just past **Stalden**, 7km south of Visp in the main valley, the side-valley splits into two: the **Mattertal** (with Zermatt and its Matterhorn) and the **Saastal** (with Saas Fee), the two most visited valleys in the Valais. On

your way to Zermatt at the end of the Mattertal you pass the village of **Randa**, where you can still see the wounds of one of the worst landslides in the Alps. In 1991, around 18th April, 14 million cubic metres of rock came down the mountains. When geologists examined the area they discovered further cracks and predicted a second catastrophe — which happened less than a month later, on the 9th of May, when another 15 million cubic metres thundered into the valley floor. **Zermatt** itself is a car-free village; you park in Täsch and go on by train.

Visp • Saas Fee (Saastal)

Visp to Saas Fee: 26km/16mi; 35min driving one way
Saas Grund to the Mattmark Dam: 11km/7mi; 23min driving one way
En route: Walk 30
Drive from Visp to **Stalden**, then turn left into the **Saastal**. In **Saas Grund**, the road forks. Continuing straight on leads to the **Mattmark Dam** (via **Saas Almagell**). Turning right brings you to car-free **Saas Fee** (all parking is in a huge multi-storey car park on the outskirts). Known as the 'pearl of the Alps', Saas Fee is set some 250m above the Saaser Vispa stream in a fantastic cirque of 4000m peaks; see the short walks on pages 168-169 to explore the area.

Sion • Lac de Derborence

22km/14mi; 35min driving one way
Derborence is the site of other landslides which took place in 1714 and 1749. The story of a shepherd buried in the rockfall inspired the novel *Derborence* by Swiss writer C F Ramuz,

published in 1934 and made into a film in 1985. Take exit 25 off the A9 motorway and follow signs to CONTHEY. Past **Conthey**, Sensine, Erde and **Aven** you're in a wild valley with numerous curves and tunnels. The road is good, but you must drive carefully. Of course there is yet another dam ahead, opposite the small and romantic **Lac de Derborence** (1449m) on the far side of the valley.

Sion • Col du Sanetsch • Sanetschsee

38km/24mi; 1h driving one way
From either exit 25 or 26 off the A9 motorway, get on cantonal route 9 towards CONTHEY. At the **Pont-de-la-Morge**, head north on Route de la Morge (a left turn before the bridge if coming from exit 25, a right just past the bridge from exit 26). After only a few metres, turn right and then immediately left on the Route

de Vuisse. Continue to **Chandolin** and from there take the Route du Sanetsch. The **Col du Sanetsch** (2251m) is snow-free from June to October. From the pass it's another 4km to the **Sanetschsee** (lake and dam, 2034m).

Sion • Lac de Tseuzier

22km/14mi; 40min driving one way
Take exit 27 off the A9 motorway (SION EST). Cross the Rhône and turn right on route 9. After 700m, bear left (Route de Molignon). Go through Argnoud and, at **Ayent**, branch off to **Lac de Tseuzier** with the Rawil Dam.

Sierre • Crans-Montana

15km/9mi; 30min driving one way
En route: Walk 26
Crans-Montana is one of the hippest holiday destinations in Switzerland. It not only offers

world-class skiing, but is also home of the European Masters golf championship. All this in a fantastic and sunny setting. You can drive there from Sierre either via Chermignon or via Venthône and Mollens.

Susten • Leukerbad
17km/11mi; 30min driving one way
From Susten on route 9 south of Leuk, a road leads to **Leukerbad** (1411m), one of the major Alpine spa resorts. In winter, you can swim in the open-air hot-water pool, surrounded by snow-covered mountains. From Leukerbad you could take a cable car either to the **Torrentalp** area (great view of the Rhône Valley and surrounding 4000m peaks; www.torrent.ch) or to the **Gemmipass** (2350m; www.gemmi.ch) for views to Monte Rosa, the Matterhorn, Weisshorn and the Bernese Alps. There's also a magnificent hiking trail from Leukerbad to the Gemmipass.

Lötschental
Gampel to Fafleralp: 22km/14mi; 30min driving one way
En route: Walk 31
The Lötschental is one of the most beautiful valleys in the Valais, largely unspoiled by the skiing circus. To get there, take the road 20km east of **Sierre**, which leads via **Gampel**, a town in the Rhône Valley, to **Goppenstein**, location of the Lötschberg Tunnel — a railway tunnel which transports passengers from and to the Bernese uplands (see page 63). Continue up the valley through the four Lötschental villages of **Ferden**, **Kippel** (**M**), which hosts the Lötschentaler Museum, **Wiler** and **Blatten**. You can drive as far as **Fafleralp**, the start/end-point of a famous high ridge path (Walk 31).

Bettmeralp
En route: Walk 32
Neither a valley nor a pass, **Bettmeralp** is a small car-free resort high above the Rhône, only accessible by cable car. It's the starting point for one of the best walks in this book, allowing you to see the **Aletsch Glacier** in its full glory. From **Brig** continue towards Furka, Grimsel, Nufenen (three major passes). In **Mörel** (7km from Brig) do *not* take the small road up to Betten (hardly any parking) but continue on the main road another 3km to reach the valley station of two cable cars (very large car park) which go to Bettmeralp, one directly, the other with a stop in Betten.

In the Lötschen Valley (Walk 31)

Touring by train

The train is an excellent way to discover Switzerland's magnificent landscapes, and some of its routes are truly spectacular. Connections are synchronized, and if you need to change trains, you can often catch the corresponding train simply on the other side of the same platform.

For more information about rail passes and a downloadable map of the public transport system (trains, buses, cable cars, funiculars, boats) see the 'Getting there and getting about' chapter starting on page 8. Below are some journeys you might enjoy — not only by rail, but by cable car or gondola.

GENEVA • ZERMATT

The line from Geneva to Zermatt (via Visp) is a very important and busy one — and it passes through stunning scenery. Depending on the train, the journey takes 3-4h. You can get on this train straight from Geneva airport. From Geneva to Lausanne, the train traverses the rolling vineyards bordering Lake Geneva (called La Côte), with occasional glimpses of the lake and, depending on visibility, the Alps. From the Lausanne railway station, the line descends to lake-level and runs via Vevey and Montreux — beside the water most of the way. The sloping vineyard terraces between Lausanne and Vevey often stretch right down to the shore of the lake; they became a UNESCO World Heritage Site in 2007. Some of the most beautiful train trips in Switzerland start from Vevey and Montreux (see page 57). The train leaves the lakeside once past Villeneuve, running almost due south from Aigle to Martigny, parallel with the Rhône. Then the train traverses the broad valley of the Valais, with Martigny, Sion, Sierre and Visp being the main towns. In December 2007 Visp became an important interchange with the new train line through the Lötschberg Basis Tunnel (see page 63). You change trains in Visp, taking a different line up the Matter Valley to Zermatt.

JURA RAILWAYS
Geneva • Yverdon-les-Bains • Neuchâtel • Biel/Bienne • Delémont • Basel

This is the main line between Geneva and Basel. On this trip you can enjoy especially beautiful vistas across Lake Neuchâtel and Lake Biel. And at intermediate stops (some of which are listed below, starting from the Geneva end of the line), trains branch off into the Jura Mountains, often through spectacular scenery.

Nyon • La Cure

Nyon is on the main line service between Geneva and Lausanne. The line to La Cure (hourly service) first runs through vineyards, then forest. Stops are St-Cergue, La Givrine, La Cure (on the border with France). This is the train to take for Walk 7 (alight at La Givrine).

Morges • L'Isle
This is a line off the beaten track, but leading through pleasant farming country, interspersed with woods. Service is every 1-2h. Shortly after leaving Morges, one of Switzerland's most beautiful castles, the Château de Vufflens, can be seen (not open to the public). The penultimate station (Mont-richer) can be used as a starting point for ascending Mont Tendre (Walk 8), the highest mountain in the Swiss Jura.

Yverdon • Ste-Croix
Another astonishing line that sees the train meandering up the Jura: whether it's the U-turn to bypass the village of Baulmes, the ascent of the Gorges de Covatanne, or the great views to the Alps, you will enjoy it. Sit on the right. Runs hourly; 36min ride. Ste-Croix can be used as a starting point for Mount Chasseron (Walk 9).

Neuchâtel • Travers • Môtiers • Fleurier • Buttes
This line leads through the Val de Travers — the beautiful valley of the Areuse River, a faithful companion from just after the town of Bôle all the way to the terminus of Buttes, with the Areuse Gorge being the most spectacular part. Sit on the left. Runs hourly; 45min ride. Get off at Môtiers for Walk 9 and in Champ du Moulin for Walk 10.

Neuchâtel • La Chaux-de-Fonds
The train passes through vineyard country and woods, with good views of Lake Neuchâtel and the Alps as it tackles the steep slopes. In Chambrelien, the locomotive changes ends. Trains run about twice an hour and take either 28min or 39min. There is also a rail line from Biel/Bienne to La-Chaux-de-Fonds (41min or 57min).

TRAINS IN THE SWISS RIVIERA REGION (VEVEY, MONTREUX)
There are a number of short train rides departing from Vevey and Montreux. Two further tourist train journeys leaving from Montreux are described below (the Golden-Pass Line and the Chocolate Train).

Vevey • Mont Pèlerin
Vevey's mountain is Mont Pèlerin, a plateau high above the town with a wonderful view. A funicular runs from Vevey, traversing the vineyards of the Lake Geneva region, up to a terrace at 806m, from where there are fine views across the lake. The lower station, called 'Vevey-Funi' (389m), is some 15min on foot from the main railway station, not far from the Nestlé headquarters. Or you can take either bus 1 or the S31 urban train from the main railway station (just one stop) to Vevey-Funi. The funicular takes 11min and runs 3-4 times an hour. From the mountain station of the funicular you can walk in just over an hour to the forest-covered summit of Mont Pèlerin (1080m), with its 'Plein Ciel' TV tower (see Car tour 1).

Vevey • Blonay • Les Pléiades
A steep and winding train ride takes you from Vevey's main station (platform 7) to Les Pléiades (change in Blonay), a fine lookout point at 1360m. Runs hourly; 40min ride. The terminus of Les Pléiades is only a couple of minutes from the summit.

Blonay • Chamby
Railway enthusiasts should not miss the short (3.2km) steam train ride between Blonay and Chamby. In Chaulin, near Chamby, there's a depot and museum (**M (** 021 943 21 21) which is home to a large collection of metre-gauge steam and electric locomotives. Trains operate Saturdays and Sundays from May through September (www.blonay-chamby.ch).

Vevey • Chexbres • Puidoux ('Train des Vignes')
This hourly train, painted yellow and blue, runs through steep vineyards between Vevey's main railway station and Puidoux (13min); it stops in Chexbres, starting point for Walk 4.

Montreux • Rochers de Naye ('Train des Marmottes')
Montreux's mountain is the Rochers de Naye. A specta-cular train ride from Montreux (400m) climbs to the summit of the Rochers de Naye (2045m). At the terminus there is a small park with different species of marmots, hence the name. The outlook from the viewing platform, a 10min walk from the terminus, is stunning — you look out over Lake Geneva and towards the Swiss and French Alps as well as the Jura. Trains run hourly from platform 8 in Montreux; it's a 55min ride. Sit on the right. Jaman station (two stations before the terminus) is the starting point for Walk 6.

Montreux/Territet • Glion
Territet is a suburb of Montreux. The Territet funicular station is a two-minute walk from Territet's main railway station. It runs every 15min and takes 4min; in Glion, you could also board the train to the Rochers de Naye.

GOLDENPASS LINE
Montreux • Zweisimmen • Interlaken • Lucerne
The stretch Montreux– Château-d'Oex– Gstaad– Zweisimmen– Spiez– Interlaken–Brünig Pass– Lucerne is one of Switzerland Tourism's most promoted train journeys, marketed under the name GoldenPass Line. It comprises three sections: Montreux– Zweisimmen (62km), Zweisimmen- –Interlaken (50km), and Interlaken–Lucerne (73km). You have to change trains in Zweisimmen and Interlaken because the rail line between these two stations is a different gauge.
The GoldenPass Line currently comprises GoldenPass Classic and GoldenPass Panoramic. The section Montreux– Zweisimmen operates two different kinds of panoramic train, one with observation cars at each end and eight VIP seats each, so that passengers have an unobstructed view ahead (the driver's cab is elevated) or behind, and the other without VIP seating. The GoldenPass Panoramic

between Montreux and Zweisimmen with VIP seats is the most popular of the GoldenPass rides. GoldenPass Panoramic trains between Zweisimmen and Interlaken have first class saloon coaches, and from Interlaken to Lucerne trains have first class cars and cars with large windows. GoldenPass Panoramic trains run three to five times a day.

The GoldenPass Classic runs between Montreux and Zweisimmen in new Belle Epoque coaches, a wine cellar coach and a dining car.

For further information see www.mob.ch or www.goldenpass.ch, (from within Switzerland: 0900 245 245; international 00 41 840 245 245.

Of course, normal trains with regular coaches also ply these routes. The website www.sbb.ch displays the schedules of all the trains.

CHOCOLATE TRAIN
Montreux • Gruyères • Broc

This one-day tourist excursion comprises an out-and-back train ride with visits to a cheese factory in Gruyères and a chocolate factory in Broc. Trains depart from Jun-Oct every Mon/Wed/Fri morning; in Jul/Aug they run Mon-Fri. Passengers travel exclusively first class, either in Belle Epoque or modern panoramic coaches.

TRAINS IN THE CHABLAIS REGION (AIGLE, BEX)
Aigle • Leysin

A cog railway connects Aigle to Leysin, a winter and summer sports resort. The train starts at Aigle's main railway station, winds its way through town like a tram, then reverses direction on a horse-shoe bend and starts the steep climb to Leysin, passing vine-yards and forest. Runs hourly; 22min ride.

Aigle • Sépey • Les Diablerets

This train also runs through town at first, then passes the castle of Aigle. In Les Planches (which is just a junction), trains make a quick detour to Le Sépey, a small resort, then return to Les Planches and continue to the village of Les Diablerets. Runs hourly; 48min ride. From the village a bus goes to the Col du Pillon, starting point for Walk 15.

Aigle • Ollon • Monthey • Champéry

The train heads south from Aigle, then climbs to the village of Ollon in vineyard country, descends again and crosses the Rhône River. In Monthey, the train reverses. From there it's a steep climb through the Val d'Illiez to Champéry. Sit on the right (there is no need to change to the other side in Monthey, even though the train reverses). Runs hourly; the ride takes about an hour.

Bex • Villars-sur-Ollon • Col de Bretaye

Bex is a 6min train ride south from Aigle. The train from Bex leads to Villars, a winter and summer resort. From Villars a cog railway climbs up to the Col de Bretaye at 2200m. Runs every hour; 40min ride.

MONT BLANC EXPRESS AND SAINT-BERNARD EXPRESS (MARTIGNY)
Mont Blanc Express: Martigny • Le Châtelard, with side-trip to Lake Emosson

A spectacular mountain railway departs from Martigny to Le Châtelard, the last station on Swiss soil before entering France and continuing to Chamonix and St-Gervais. From Martigny station, the train runs in the Rhône Valley to Vernayaz where the steep climb (20%) to the next stop, Salvan, starts. The most dizzying part of the trip begins in Le Trétien, traversing a number of tunnels and bridges, with a drop of over 400m to the valley floor. The village of Finhaut is frequented by hikers. Le Châtelard marks the end point of the Swiss part of the trip.

Mountain railway and funicular aficionados will love the excursion to Lake Emosson (www.chatelard.net): from Le Châtelard, first take the incredibly steep funicular (88%) for 12min to the Station du Château d'Eau (1822m). Then board a 60cm-gauge train which brings you in 12min to the foot of the Emosson Dam. The third (and last!) stretch is a funicular, the Minifunic (2min), to La Gueulaz (1965m) near the top of the dam. The dam offers a great view of Mont Blanc (4810m), the highest mountain in the Alps.

Saint-Bernard Express: Martigny to Le Châble (for Verbier) or Orsières (for the Grand St-Bernard Pass)

This train departs from Martigny and passes through the Val d'Entremont to Sembrancher, where the track divides to reach either Orsières or Le Châble (trains usually run direct to Orsières, with passengers for Le Châble having to change in Sembrancher). From Le Châble, you can reach the world-famous ski resort of Verbier either by bus or by cable car.

From Orsières you have the choice of three destinations which can be reached by bus:
(1) You can make for Champex-Lac, a resort with an idyllic lake.
(2) You can travel up the quiet valley of Val Ferret, starting point of numerous hikes; the terminus is Ferret (summer only).
(3) For a truly historic trip, continue along the same valley, the Val d'Entremont, travelling via Bourg-St-Pierre to the hospice on the Grand St-Bernard Pass (open June to October), where Walk 22 starts.

RAILWAYS, CABLE CARS AND GONDOLAS IN THE JUNGFRAU REGION
Interlaken Ost • Wilderswil • Zweilütschinen • Grindelwald or Lauterbrunnen

Trains leaving Interlaken Ost railway station bound for Lauterbrunnen and Grindelwald separate into two sections at Zweilütschinen — one going to Grindelwald (Walks 16-19), the other to Lauterbrunnen (Walk 20). Make sure you sit in the correct section of the train when you board at Interlaken or Wilderswil!

Grindelwald or Lauterbrunnen • Kleine Scheidegg • Jungfraujoch

Kleine Scheidegg (2061m) comprises a busy railway

station and a few hotels and restaurants amidst pastures with herds of cows. It's a departure point for climbers who tackle the dangerous north face of the Eiger, hikers who take the Eigertrail (Walk 18) or visitors who board the train to go up to the Jungfraujoch at 3454m. Kleine Scheidegg can be reached either from Lauterbrunnen or from Grindelwald.

If you travel from Grindelwald main station you need to change trains and board the WAB train (Wengernalp-Bahn) which descends to Grindelwald-Grund. The train then reverses and begins its ascent to Kleine Scheidegg, passing directly beneath the north face of the Eiger (to your left). Sit on the left when boarding at Grindelwald main station, so that after the train changes direction in Grindelwald-Grund, you will be on the right-hand side to enjoy beautiful views across pastures.

If you take the route via Lauterbrunnen, the train meanders to Wengen (1274m), a car-free summer and winter resort, home of the world-famous Alpine ski race, the Lauberhorn Descent, with

Funicular towards the Reichenbach Falls (see Car tour 6)

splendid views to the Staub-bach waterfalls and the grandiose Jungfrau massif. From Wengen, the train continues via Wengernalp to Kleine Scheidegg. Sit on the right. From Wengen there is also a gondola to Mount Männlichen.

At Kleine Scheidegg you may well be asking yourself which is more admirable — the crazy idea of building a railway line inside a mountain up to the pass of Jungfraujoch at 3454m, or the engineering feat which took 16 years to complete (1896 to 1912). The Jung-fraubahn is 9.3km long and traverses only two tunnels, one of which is 7.12km long. You board the train to the Jung-fraujoch at Kleine Scheidegg. After the first station, Eiger-gletscher (Eiger glacier; 2320m), the train vanishes into a tunnel and stays in the tunnel all the way to the Jungfraujoch (3454m). From this pass there is a magnificent view down the Aletsch Glacier. The Jung-fraubahn operates all year round (every 30min from mid-June till October, otherwise every hour). Before you take this trip, make sure that visibility will be good, and wear warm clothing.

Lauterbrunnen • Mürren • Schilthorn
Mount Schilthorn offers one of the best views in the Alps. There are various routes to get to the top of Schilthorn. Two use mechanical help, the third is on foot, Walk 20 — in combination with cable cars and trains.
(1) Either take the post bus from Lauterbrunnen to almost the head of the valley (Stechel-berg Schilthornbahn; bus runs every 30min to 1h; 16min ride), or walk (see Car tour 6, short walk on page 42), then take the cable car up Mount Schilthorn in four stages — via the car-free villages of Gimmelwald and Mürren, Mount Birg, and finally Schilthorn (32min).
(2) From Lauterbrunnen, take the cable car to Grütschalp (1480m), from where a train will take you to Mürren (14min) — a short ride, but with tremendous views. Sit on the left.

Wilderswil • Schynige Platte
From Wilderswil, on the Interlaken–Grindelwald/Lauterbrunnen line, a train snakes up through forest via Breitlauenen to the terminus Schynige Platte (1967m) — a station with what must be one of the world's most gorgeous views. At the end of Walk 16, you take the train in the reverse direction, from Schynige Platte to Wilderswil (runs mid-June to October, roughly hourly).

Grindelwald • Mount First
A two-section gondola runs from Grindelwald (1061m) to First (2166m). The Grindel-wald gondola station is about a 10min walk (east) from Grindelwald's main railway station. The mountain station is the starting point of a popular hike (Walk 16).

Grindelwald • Mount Männlichen
West of Grindelwald, a 6.2km-long gondola ride whisks you in 30min from Grindelwald-Grund to the mountain station (2224m) of Männlichen, the starting point for one of the most popular walks in the Alps (Walk 19).

RAILWAYS, COG RAILWAYS AND CABLE CARS IN ZERMATT
Gornergrat

Thanks to the Matterhorn, the Gornergratbahn, a cog railway, is Switzerland's most popular mountain railway. Views are good on both the left and the right. There are four intermediate stops: Findelbach (1770m), Riffelalp (2211m), Riffelberg (2582m) and Rotenboden (2815m), before it reaches the top at Gornergrat (3092m). Runs throughout the year (except from mid-October to November); 2-3 trips per hour; 38min ride. Walk 29 sets off from Gornergrat.

Unterrothorn

Sunneggabahn is an underground funicular from Zermatt to Sunnegga (2288m, 3min). From there a gondola takes you to Blauherd (2571m) and then a cable car to Unterrothorn (3104m). About 30min.

Klein Matterhorn

Cable cars run from Zermatt to Furi (1867m), then on to Trockener Steg (2939m), and finally to Klein Matterhorn (3883m).

Schwarzsee

From Zermatt, take the cable car to Furi, then the one from Furi to Schwarzsee, a lake at 2552m.

GLACIER EXPRESS
Zermatt • St-Moritz

The Glacier Express is Switzerland's most popular tourist train. With an average speed of 36km/h, it is advertised as the slowest express train in the world. The trip lasts about 8h. Trains run throughout the year, two-three times a day in each direction. There are special coaches with panoramic windows. Seat reservations are mandatory.

LÖTSCHBERG TUNNEL AND LÖTSCHBERG BASIS TUNNEL

Two of Switzerland's most impressive engineering feats are the tunnels which have been pierced through the mountains to connect the Bernese Oberland with the Valais: the Lötschberg Tunnel and the Lötschberg Basis Tunnel.

The Lötschberg Tunnel was constructed 1906-1912; trains enter this tunnel in Kandersteg and emerge after 9.4km in Goppenstein.

The Lötschberg Basis Tunnel, 400m below the Lötschberg Tunnel (therefore the German name 'Basis', indicating base or lower), opened in 2007. Trains vanish into the mountain in Frutigen and resurface after 34.6km in Raron in the Valais. This is the longest land tunnel in the world.

Both tunnels are rail-only. The old Lötschberg Tunnel transports passengers seated in their cars — just a 15min trip (www.loetschberg.ch). The Lötschberg Basis Tunnel transports goods and has coaches for passengers, but does not take cars.

☀ Walking

Switzerland offers a myriad of hiking possibilities. The walks in this guide have been selected because they are accessible both by car *and* public transport — which still gave me a huge choice! Some routes in the guide rank among the world's top hiking destinations, others may only be known to those walking *aficionados* who live in the region. However, in the end it doesn't really matter where you set off: you will find natural beauty all around you.

Most of the walks in this book are *circuits,* some are *out-and-back* the same way, and a few are *linear* (in which case you can return to your starting point by public transport).

There are 32 *main walks,* from easy to very strenuous. But you will have a choice of almost 100 shorter versions or alternative routes. In addition, a further 36 short rambles, especially suited to motorists, are suggested in Car tours 1-7. (Car tour 8 explores the fascinating side-valleys of the Valais, where 11 of the main walks — and their shorter versions — are located.) Whether you'd like to do leisurely rambling or serious hiking, you will have **more than 150 walks** from which to choose.

Routes and waymarking

Hiking routes, signposting and waymarking are standardized in most of Switzerland. Most commonly, destination, walking time and altitude are indicated (see photographs opposite and on page 175). (Zermatt has its own standard; a typical signpost there can be seen in the photograph on page 163.) There are three types of route:

• **Walking route** (*Wanderweg* in German, *chemin pédestre* or *itinéraire pédestre* in French): easy paths through hills or along the lower mountain slopes. Marked entirely in yellow, either as a directional marker at junctions, or as a rhombus (see photograph on pages 96-97) to indicate that you are still on the right track.

• **Mountain route** (*Bergwanderweg* in German, *itinéraire de montagne* in French): paths through rougher territory. Signs have a yellow body with a white-red-white arrowhead. Hiking boots are always required.

- **Alpine route** (*Alpinwanderweg* in German, *itinéraire alpin* in French): these include glacier traverses and light climbing. Alpine equipment is required. Signs are in blue, with a white-blue-white arrowhead.

Hikes in this guide follow routes from the first two categories only — with very minor exceptions (Walks 19 and 32 describe Alpine routes as Alternative walks). Waymarking in Switzerland is excellent. Still, nature is dynamic, and landslides, floods or avalanches may force you to re-route.

A forest of signposts in Ste-Croix (Walk 9); the location and altitude are shown on the white ground, various destinations and walking times on the fingerposts. The brown fingerpost indicates an historic site or route.

The **spelling of names** on maps and signposts may at times differ in Swiss-German areas (rarely in French-speaking Switzerland). The Swiss-Germans use High German as a formal language (eg in newspapers), but the native language is Swiss-German (Schwyzer Dütsch) which, depending on the dialect, might not be understood at all by Germans. For example, whereas the name on the official Swiss mapping reads *Trochni Stäge* (Swiss-German), the name on the signpost is *Trockene Stiege* (High German). Swiss French is basically identical to the French spoken in France. French and German geographical names often differ.

Grading

The **walking times** given in this book are approximate values and *do not include breaks.* If you are fit, you will be faster. None of the walks demand climbing equipment. Some of the walks require that you are sure-footed, and a couple that you have a head for heights. The **ascent** indicated under 'Grade' at the start of each walk is not necessarily the difference between the highest and lowest elevation of the walk, but *includes intermittent ascents as well.* Ascent and descent are the same for both circular and out-and back walks; for linear walks, both ascent and descent are given.

Seasons

You can walk in Switzerland **all year round**, though not all destinations can be reached throughout the year. Up to around **2000m** the mountains are snow-free by May/June. For mountains rising **2500m and higher**, July to September are the best months for hiking. In the mountains, the summer hiking season runs from June to October. **Mountain huts** are generally open from June to September and for the winter skiing season from mid-December to mid-April. *In between those periods many mountain resorts close down.*

Walks close to the shore of **Lake Geneva** (Walks 2-5) can be done in any season; snowfall is rare, and if it snows, it usually stays just a couple of days. The best months for walks in the **Jura** (Walks 7-12) are May to October/November; in the winter time, while some of them would be dangerous (eg the gorge walk sections of Walks 9 or 11), others can be undertaken with snowshoes. Walk 13 in the **Gruyère** region can also be done when there is some snow. In the **Valais**, if you stay in the valley, Walk 21 through the vineyards is suitable any time of year. All other walks in the Valais and in the Bernese uplands are only for the summer.

Although **winter walking** is a marvelous experience, with visibility being at its best and numerous mountain resorts preparing paths for walkers, *this guide assumes snow-free conditions.* A harmless path in the summer under dry conditions can easily become a dangerous undertaking in the winter.

Maps

The hiking maps in this book, together with the generally excellent signposting and waymarking, will be sufficient to help you find your way. However, if you plan to go further afield, obtain the relevant maps. The maps in this book are based on the official mapping of the Federal Office of Topography (www.swisstopo.ch, with English pages). They offer the following maps:
• 1:25,000: printed maps — minute detail, but they do not highlight hiking routes;
• 1:50,000: printed maps showing hiking routes;
• 1:25,000 *on DVD:* '**Swiss Map 25**' includes the national map at 1:500,000 plus the 1:25,000 series. Although expensive, it includes the complete official Swiss footpath network and lets you calculate elevation profiles and determine walking times (but take them with a grain of salt...). Routes may be uploaded to Garmin and Magellan GPS units. All of Switzerland is covered by eight DVDs (available for both Mac and PC). If you are doing extended hiking, this is an excellent product.

The publisher Hallwag Kümmerly + Frey also covers Switzerland with 32 sheets, most of them at 1:60,000. Tourist offices often have hiking maps as well.

Below is a **key** to the walking maps in this guide.

E41	motorway	– 400 –	height in metres		castle, fort.hotel
	trunk road		waterfall, spring, etc		mountain inn.hut
	main road		power station		restaurant. refreshments
	secondary road		church.chapel		
	minor road		shrine/cross.cemetery		specified building
	unsurfaced road		picnic tables	M	museum
	track, path, trail		best views		monument.tower
	main walk		bus stop.car parking		cave.signpost
	alternative walk		railway station		transmitter.stadium
WALKING	*other waymarked*		funicular railway		rock formation
MOUNTAIN	*routes shown on the*		cable car, gondola or		orientation table
ALPINE	*maps (see page 64)*		chair lift.ski lift		map continuation

Equipment

The contents of your rucksack depend on the weather, the time of the year and the length of the walk. For more strenuous walks and for walks on mountain paths you will need:
- Hiking boots (waterproof) with ankle support,
- Walking sticks
- Backpack (30 litre)
- Clothes: fast-drying T-shirts (not cotton); even in summer take warm clothing with you when you go up to higher altitudes. When the weather turns or a wind comes up, it can get cold very quickly. Take rainproof gear and a change of clothing.
- Water (1-3 litres, depending on the length of the walk and the season)
- This guide or a map (see page 67)
- Basic first-aid kit; sun protection — cream, hat, glasses (the glaciers can be blinding)
- Photographic gear
- Mobile phone, whistle
- For overnight stays at huts: sleeping sack, provisions

Safety

Absolute safety doesn't exist in life, and certainly not in the mountains. In addition to using common sense, please consider the following advice:
- *Check the weather forecast.* Paths which are safe in dry weather can become very dangerous when wet or snow-covered. Pay particular attention to thunderstorms.
- *Watch out for falling rocks.* Make sure you do not dislodge stones from the path, and watch out for rockfall caused by walkers or animals above you.
- *Don't overestimate your own ability.*
- *Be well equipped and have enough water with you.*
- *If the weather deteriorates* or if the path makes you feel queasy — be brave and *turn back.*
- ***Note the following** important telephone numbers**
    117 Police (emergencies)
    118 Fire brigade
    144 Ambulance
    112 International emergency calls via mobile phone

*When phoning *within* Switzerland you **must always** enter the local area code; eg if calling a number in Geneva from Geneva, you have to dial the local area code 022 followed by the number. If you are calling Switzerland from *outside* the country, the country code is 41, and the leading 0 from the local area code is dropped.

Literature and websites

Landscapes of Lake Geneva and Western Switzerland is a *countryside guide*, intended to be used in tandem with a **general guide** of your choosing. For walkers, there are many books in German and in French, but guides in English are few. The following are all well written and researched:

Walking in the Valais and *The Bernese Alps,* both by Kev Reynolds (and both published by Cicerone) are very comprehensive, but have no maps.

Walking Switzerland, by Marcia and Philip Lieberman (The Mountaineers) covers a few areas of Switzerland in depth, but has only very schematic overview maps.

Walking in Switzerland, by Clem Lindenmayer (Lonely Planet) describes mostly linear walks, illustrated with black and white sketch maps.

Rother Verlag, the best-known German publisher of mountain guides, covers Switzerland with about 25 books of 50 walks each; a couple of them have been translated into English (see www.rother.de).

Of the plethora of **websites** devoted to Switzerland, the following two stand out:

www.myswitzerland.com: the website of Switzerland Tourism, the country's national marketing and sales organisation. This is an excellent website with tons of information, from hotels and events to hiking tours with schematic and satellite maps.

www.schweizmobil.ch: the website of Schweiz-Mobil (SwitzerlandMobility), the national network for non-motorized traffic (hiking, cycling, mountain biking, skating and canoeing). They have created over 20 national and 100 regional multi-day routes for hikers (over 6000km), (mountain) bikers, skaters and canoeists. These routes are linked to a wide range of services such as overnight accommodation, rental of bicycles and offers for bookable luggage transport. In the photograph on page 65, you can see that the yellow fingerposts have been supplemented by green route information panels including route names and numbers (5 and 70 in the photo). These are SwitzerlandMobility signs (1-digit numbers for national, 2-digit numbers for regional and 3-digit numbers for local routes). Information is provided on the internet as well as in guides and maps.

Hikers are spoiled in Switzerland!

Walk 1 (Lake Geneva): SALEVE, GENEVA'S MOUNTAIN IN FRANCE

Distance/time: 7km/4.3mi; 3h10min

Best period: any time of year, as long as ice and snow don't make the paths dangerous

Grade: easy, except for the few minutes on the La Corraterie balcony path (shown overleaf), where you need a head for heights. Alternatively, skip La Corraterie and retrace your steps. Ascent a little over 300m/1000ft; highest point 1309m, lowest 1097m

Equipment: hiking boots — and best to take your *passport!*

Refreshments/accommodation: several restaurants on the way: La Table d'Orientation; TV tower Restaurant de l'Observatoire; three restaurants in the village of La Croisette. Plenty of hotels in Geneva, but during world-famous events such as the Geneva Motor Show in March or ITU Telecom, Geneva and its surroundings are booked out.

Transport: city  8 (Veyrier-Douane) from just in front of Geneva's railway station (Gare Cornavin) to its terminus (30min). (This line alternates with another line 8 bus, Veyrier-Tournettes. The two lines split at the station called Sierne, from where you can walk in 15min to the terminus of Veyrier-Douane — or wait the same amount of time for the next bus.) From Veyrier-Douane it's just 150m to the French border (passports needed). Walk for 10min to the ⛫ station (430m) and take the cable car up Salève. The cable car currently runs May-Sep daily, Apr and Oct daily except Monday, Jan-Mar weekends only; departs every 12min; (00 33 4 50 39 86 86, www.telepheriquedusaleve. com. 🚘: A40 motorway in France, from Annemasse towards St-Julien; park in the motorway lay-by called Téléphérique du Salève (🚡).

S alève is a mountain-lovers' paradise: on Geneva's doorstep but rising in France, this elongated mountain ridge offers something for everyone — strollers, hikers, bikers, climbers, *via ferrata aficionados* … even couch potatoes, since it can be mastered by car and cable car. If you took a different hike on Salève every weekend, they would keep you going all year. Even though the highest point is a modest 1379m, Salève offers tremendous vistas to the Jura and the Alps with Mont Blanc, and a splendid view down over Geneva with its landmark fountain, the Jet d'Eau, in the lake. Every inhabitant of the city who makes it up Salève tries to identify his or her apartment from up there.

From the **Salève mountain station** of the cable car (1097m), take the sloping path rising to the right. You cross the road twice, pass a paragliding take-off point and arrive at the restaurant La

Table d'Orientation (1211m, **20min**) from which you have a splendid view over Geneva. Continue climbing; a TV tower is not far off to the left (signpost L'OBSERVATOIRE, 1244m, **30min**).
You pass the signposts GRANDE GORGE NORD (1250m, **35min**) and GRANDE GORGE SUD (1286m, **45min**). Keep straight ahead on the clearly visible track through pastures, still ascending slightly. At the signpost ALT 1300m (**55min**) in the middle of the pasture, make a quick detour 90° to the left and walk to an excellent ORIENTATION TABLE with the names of all the mountains you can see (20min there and back).
Return to the ALT 1300m sign (**1h15min**) and continue south, now descending slightly and passing another paragliding take-off point (**1h25min**). On reaching the road (**1h30min**), walk 130m downhill to the signpost LES

On the plateau of Salève, with Mont Blanc in the background

La Corraterie balcony path

The following 10 minutes, on the high ridge path (**La Corraterie**) are quite exposed but technically easy. Afterwards the path runs through woods and passes a signpost ALT 1220m (**2h25min**). When the path touches the road again (1286m; **2h 30min**), retrace your outward path to the **mountain station** (**3h10min**) and take the cable car back to Veyrier. Alternatively, you can walk down (a descent of 670m, taking 1h40min). From the mountain station, descend a signposted path — at times steepish — to the village of Monnetier (700m). At the church, turn left and follow the road into the Pas d'Echelle, a path hewn from the rock and secured by railings (steep, but not technically difficult). This leads back to the valley station of the cable car.

CRETS (1214m). If you're not going to continue to the hamlet of **La Croisette** (1175m) for a break in one of the three restaurants (20min return), make a sharp right turn here, on a downward-sloping, narrow path. Ten minutes later, at the signpost ORJOBET (1200m, **1h40min**), continue straight on. Two minutes later, go straight over a junction, climb a couple of zigzags and then pass a big hole in the rock (**Trou de la Tine, 1h50min**).

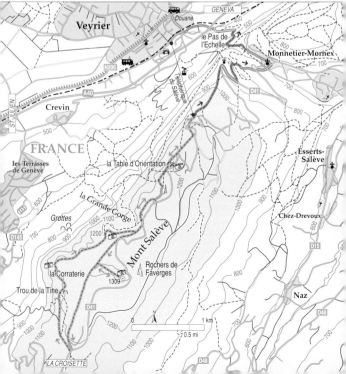

Walk 2 (Lake Geneva): VINEYARDS OF DARDAGNY

Distance/time: about 12km/7.4mi; 3h35min from Dardagny; 4h20min from La Plaine

Best period: any time of year; particularly beautiful during the autumn grape harvest.

Grade: easy from Dardagny. But if you take the train to La Plaine to start the walk, there's a short but very steep ascent not far after leaving the railway station. Otherwise the walk, mostly on surfaced roads, undulates gently, with an overall ascent of about 250m/820ft (highest point 500m, lowest 387m). The stretch through the Vallon de Roulave is slippery when wet, and the wine nature trail is not waymarked (follow the notes carefully).

Equipment: hiking books for the Vallon de Roulave in wet conditions, otherwise trainers.

Refreshments/accommodation: restaurant at the Auberge de Dardagny, (022 754 14 72; Auberge Restaurant des Granges, (022 754 16 00,

www.lesgranges.ch, closed Dec-Feb, three B&B rooms. Drinking-water fountains in Essertines, Malval and Dardagny.

Transport: 🚋 from Geneva Cornavin (the main railway station) to La Plaine, daily, hourly from 6am till midnight, journey time 25min. Then on foot to Dardagny: from the station walk along the railway tracks (waymarked) for about 300m, to a crossing track (closed to vehicles but waymarked for walkers), cross the railway tracks here and, after a short but steep ascent, reach the Salle Polyvalente (multi-purpose hall) and its car park just outside Dardagny (25min). 🚗 to Dardagny; park in the car park at the above-mentioned Salle Polyvalente just outside Dardagny.

Shorter walks: There are numerous ways to shorten the walk, for instance, only do the wine nature trail or the Vallon de l'Allondon, or parts thereof.

This hike comprises two parts: the vineyards of Geneva and the natural reserve of Allondon. The undulating vineyards contrast strongly with the surrounding mountains of the Jura. Traditional wines are here are Chasselas and Gamay, but increasingly one finds Chardonnay, Müller-Thurgau, Pinot blanc, Aligoté, Sauvignon blanc, Pinot gris, Gamaret, Merlot, Garanoir, Cabernet Sauvignon and Cabernet franc in the canton of Geneva. The wine nature trail has 21 display boards (in French). This hike touches on the border with France, but does not cross it.

At the car park for the SALLE POLYVALENTE in **Dardagny** (428m) there is an INFORMATION BOARD showing the itinerary of the wine nature trail. Walk 20m from the board alongside the TENNIS COURTS, turn right and go between the field and the meadow for 100m, to reach the FIRST VINEYARD. Turn right for 50+m, left for 100+m, then right again for 200m, to reach a surfaced road which descends from Dardagny. Follow this to the left, crossing

73

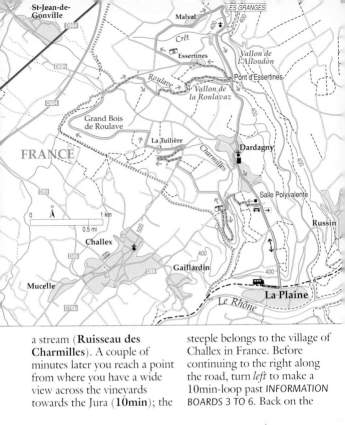

a stream (**Ruisseau des Charmilles**). A couple of minutes later you reach a point from where you have a wide view across the vineyards towards the Jura (**10min**); the steeple belongs to the village of Challex in France. Before continuing to the right along the road, turn *left* to make a 10min-loop past *INFORMATION BOARDS 3 TO 6*. Back on the

road (**20min**), walk from this junction to the next one (**23min**) and turn left, slightly uphill. At the next junction turn right, curving gently upward, ignoring the next road to the right.

When you reach another road (**40min**), fork right and, 100m further on, take another detour through vineyards (INFORMATION BOARDS 10 TO 14). Cross a stream (**50min**) and turn left. Pass through the hamlet of **La Tuilière** (482m, **55min**). At the next intersection go right, and after 200m left. You now leave the vineyards and follow the forest road which traverses the **Grand Bois de Roulave**. When you reach a country road (**1h30min**), turn right, follow it upwards for 150m, then branch left on a trail descending through forest. You cross a further stream and reach another country road (**1h40min**). Turn right and

follow the road for five minutes, then take the small path descending to the left. You are now traversing the **Vallon de la Roulavaz**; the path follows the stream **Roulave**. You pass two small GROTTOS and, a few minutes later, you could inspect another grotto by crossing the stream and following a path uphill. The main trail, however, continues on the left side of the rivulet. *Ignore* a path forking left (signposted to Essertines); keep by the Roulave.

Reaching the **Pont d'Essertines** (387m, **2h20min**), follow the sign for ESSERTINES and take the path going up to the left. Go through **Essertines** (455m, **2h35min**) and fork right at the junction just outside this hamlet (SIGN). The Jura mountains now seem within grasp; the peaks ahead are the highest in the (French and Swiss) Jura.

After passing through another hamlet, **Malval** (**2h50min**), turn right at an intersection (**3h**). You are now in the **Vallon de l'Allondon** (if you turn left, you'll reach the Auberge Restaurant des Granges). Passing the 13th-century **Chapelle de Malval**, you come back to the **Pont d'Essertines** (**3h10min**). Continue on the country road back to **Dardagny** (**3h25min**). Opposite the church is an unexpected treasure of a bookshop (lots of books, new and used). The castle next to the church now houses the mayor's office. Stroll through Dardagny, back to the car park at the SALLE POLYVALENTE (**3h35min**), or continue to the railway station in La Plaine.

Dardagny's church and castle through vineyards

Walk 3 (Lake Geneva): VINEYARDS OF LA COTE AND THE SIGNAL DE BOUGY

Distance/time: 10km/6.2mi; 2h40min

Best period: any time of year; particularly beautiful in autumn during grape harvest

Grade: easy; mostly on surfaced vineyard roads; ascent 330m; highest point 707m, lowest 495m

Equipment: training shoes

Refreshments: large (42ha) park for relaxation/recreation on the Signal de Bougy (great for children), with restaurant (open early Mar to early Nov; www.signaldebougy.ch).

Transport: 🚆 to Allaman railway station (Geneva–Lausanne line), then 🚌 to Aubonne's *gare* (main bus station, a 6min ride, hourly departures). 🚗 exit 14 for Aubonne off the A1 motorway to a car park diagonally opposite the main bus station, just before you enter the old town (2.2km from the motorway).

Shorter walk: between Mar-early Nov a bus runs from Rolle to the Signal de Bougy, where you could enjoy the park's woodland trails.

Alternative walks

1 Signal de Bougy from Allaman (3h30min). Start at Allaman station (422m): walk 40min to Aubonne. Leave the main walk at the 2h-point, to return to Allaman (50min). All signposted/waymarked.

2 Traverse of La Côte (6h30min; moderate ascent of 450m and descent of 550m). Follow the main walk from Aubonne to Bougy-Villars, but then turn right and continue through the scenic villages of Mont Dessus, Bugnaux, Vincy, Gilly, Bursins, Vinzel, Luins, Begnins, Coinsins and Duillier to the larger town of Nyon on Lake Geneva. This walk (*not* shown on our map, but well signposted and waymarked), can be shortened in various places: in Gilly, take the bus to Rolle or Gland; in Begnins, take the bus via Coinsins to Nyon or straight to Gland's railway station.

La Côte is the sloping north shore of Lake Geneva, stretching from Nyon to Lausanne and well known for its charming vineyards (see below) and pretty villages. From here as well as from the Signal de Bougy, a modest mountain, you enjoy fine views of the Alps.

From the main BUS STATION in **Aubonne** (508m), walk into the old town on its main road (RUE DE CHENE). Turn right after 100+m, then left after 30m. Walk up the GRANDE RUE for 200m and turn left through an archway onto a residential road, RUE DU CHAFFARD (**5min**). Cross a main road (**10min**) and continue straight on (now called ROUTE DE BOUGY) for 100+m, then turn left. After just under 200m you come to the end of the residential road; the vineyards start, and you leave the last residential areas of Aubonne behind (**15min**).

Follow the yellow signs, heading towards FÉCHY on a lane (CHEMIN DES CURZILLES, then CHEMIN DES PEYTROULES). Arriving at an intersection just before **Féchy** (**40min**), turn left to visit this picturesque village, taking in the 'Vignoble du Monde' behind the church, a small vineyard with grape vines from around the world. Then return to the intersection and continue straight ahead uphill on the Route de Bougy. Cross an intersection and continue on CHEMIN DE LA BOSSENAZ.

When you reach the forest (**50min**), turn left (still on Chemin de la Bossenaz). Past a couple of posh residences, fork right on an earthen path. Turn right at the next junction and walk on the road through the forest until the view opens up to the other side of the Signal mountain (**1h05min**). Turn left at the next intersection and follow woodland trails (forest adventure park) to the **Signal de Bougy** (707m), with a pavillon at its highest point. Walk straight ahead for 200m, to a SIGNPOST with a TELESCOPE and ORIENTATION TABLE, close to the park's restaurant (**1h20min**).

Go through the gate at the signpost and head down a path for 200m, to a surfaced road. Follow this downhill to another of La Côte's pleasant villages, **Bougy-Villars** (546m, **1h35min**), and turn left on the main village road. After 100m, be sure to stop at Tristan (www.chocolatier-tristan.ch), arguably the world's best chocolate-maker. There is another ORIENTATION TABLE at the church.

Leave Bougy-Villars by following the yellow signposts to FECHY. Back at the intersection just outside **Féchy** (**2h**), retrace your outgoing route to **Aubonne** (**2h40min**).

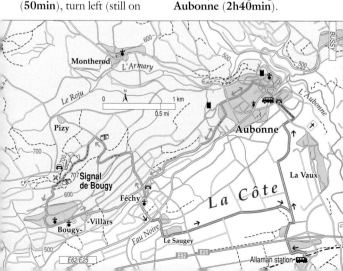

Walk 4 (Lake Geneva): LAVAUX VINEYARD TERRACES (UNESCO WORLD HERITAGE SITE)

See also photograph on pages 12-13
Distance/time: 16km/10mi 4h25min (but see Shorter walk suggestions below)
Best period: any time of year; particularly beautiful in autumn during grape harvest
Grade: easy-moderate, with an overall ascent of about 430m/1410ft (highest point 649m, lowest 375m); almost all on surfaced vineyard roads. The section where you will work up a sweat is from Epesses to La Croix: the steepest part has a gradient of 34%. Numerous benches for a rest and picnic with fine views, as well as restaurants to savour. Most of the route is way-marked in yellow; where not, details are given below.
Equipment: training shoes
Refreshments/accommodation: Hotel-Restaurant Au Major-Davel, (021 799 94 94, 12 rooms, right on the lake in Cully at the embarkation point, www.hotelaumajordavel.ch; Hotel du Signal de Chexbres (4-star), (021 946 05 05, www.hotelsignal.ch (open Mar-Nov). See also www. lavaux.ch for general information about the area.
Transport: the starting point is Chexbres. S21 from Lausanne to Puidoux-Chexbres, then S31 ('Train des Vignes', see page 58) to Chexbres-Village (14min). Or S31 direct from Vevey to Chexbres-Village (8min, runs hourly). : exit 13 for Chexbres off the A9 motorway to the car park at Chexbres railway station (about 50 places) — this gets crowded at times, but there is a smaller car park with 18 places at the Place

de Coeur d'Or, under the railway bridge off the main road.
Shorter walks: There are numerous ways to tailor this walk to your taste. In addition to the proposals below, you can begin or end the walk in Cully, Epesses, Rivaz or St-Saphorin, since some trains also stop in these small stations.
1 Eastern part only — Chexbres circuit via St-Saphorin (2h10min, ascent about 250m). Follow the main walk via St-Saphorin. In Rivaz, turn right and, after a few metres go left; follow this road up to Chexbres.
2 Western part only — Chexbres circuit via Cully (2h50min, ascent about 300m). From the railway station in Chexbres, head west to the end of the car park. Go up the ramp, take a sharp left turn over the bridge, walk around 200m downhill, and then turn right on a vineyard road. Follow this down to Rivaz (not waymarked, but you can see your goal below). At Rivaz pick up the main

Lake Geneva
(Lac Léman)

walk at the 1h50min-point and follow it to the end.

3 Main walk with shortened western portion (3h45min, ascent 380m). In Epesses (the 2h40min-point), go right, up to the main village, then pick up the main walk again just after the 3h20min-point.

Alternative walk: Lavaux Vineyard Trail (33km, 8h30min). This long-distance trail from Lausanne-Ouchy to the castle of Chillon is marked with blue signs and the lettering *GT (Grande traversée)*. The route runs Lausanne-Ouchy — Lutry — Châtelard — Villette — Grandvaux — Chenaux — Riex — Epesses — Rivaz — St-Saphorin — Chardonne — Jongny — Coisier — Vevey — Chally — Montreux — Territet — Château de Chillon. Leaflets are available in tourist offices or can be downloaded from www.lavaux.ch. *But note:* all the highlights along this trail are covered in the walk below and in Walk 5. The 'GT' trail is only worth doing from Lausanne-Ouchy to Chardonne; afterwards it traverses mostly residential areas.

Tip: A mini 'tourist train' also runs through the Lavaux region (May-Oct, (021 799 54 54; www.lavauxexpress.ch).

The local wine is a must, and so is this walk. The Lavaux vineyard terraces stretch from the eastern outskirts of Lausanne to the castle of Chillon. The terraces, at times rising very steeply up from the lake, date from the 11th century or earlier. In 2007, UNESCO declared the area 'a cultural landscape that is an outstanding example of centuries-long interaction between people and their environment, developed to optimize local resources so as to produce a highly valued wine' (whc.unesco.org). This walk traverses these terraces with their cozy little old towns, famous for wine-growing. Numerous information boards (in English) help unravel the mysteries of viticulture.

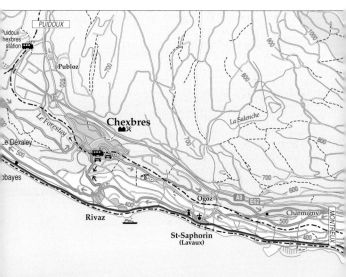

From the RAILWAY STATION in **Chexbres** (559m), go 100m east (downhill) to the main through street. Turn right, go under the RAILWAY BRIDGE and follow the main road. After 100m you come to an esplanade with an ORIENTATION TABLE (opposite the Café de la Poste). Continuing on the main road, you reach another viewpoint with an ORIENTATION TABLE (**15min**). Some 50m further on, cross the main road and take the ascending vineyard road which after a few metres goes under the RAILWAY LINE. Take CHEMIN D'OGOZ (**20min**) and then CHEMIN SOUS-OGOZ, until you come to to a junction where the yellow signs point downhill to the right (**35min**).

However, *do not* follow the signs. Instead, go straight ahead on the CHEMIN DES PEDANCES (*no* yellow signs on the next section; follow the notes carefully). After a few metres, go either left or right to round a house. After 600m the two routes merge (Charmigny on the map; **50min**). Continue for a couple of minutes and take advantage of a pleasant PICNIC AREA WITH AN OLD WINEPRESS and fountain (the latter with the inscription: *'Elle est potable mais c'est pas du Chardonnay'* — 'It's drinkable but it's not Chardonnay'). This is the most eastward point of our walk. Make a U-turn to the right here and, at the next fork (**55min**) you'll be back on a yellow-marked road (and you'll now stay on yellow-marked routes until Cully, the most westerly point of the walk). At the next intersection continue towards ST-SAPHORIN. Cross the main road (**1h15min**) which descends from Chexbres

towards the shore of the lake and come into **St-Saphorin** (405m, **1h25min**). The road (CHEMIN DU MONT) rises for about 200m, then bears left after the MEMORIAL for the local poet and singer Jean Villard Gilles. The next wine village is **Rivaz** (445m, **1h50min**). *(Shorter walk 1 turns right here for Chexbres; see page 78.)*
The main walk turns left in Rivaz; then, after a few metres, turn right. At the fountain take another right (CHEMIN DU FORESTAY), after 50m cross a bridge, then go left on CHEMIN DE LA DAME. The road ascends, and after five minutes you reach another esplanade. Here bear left and descend again. You pass the wine-growing estates of **Les Abbayes** (signpost, 431m, **2h15min**) and **Le Déxaley** (**2h20min**). At the junction 10 minutes

later bear left, to a small group of houses which belong to **Epesses** (signpost, **2h40min**). *(Shorter walk 3 turns right here, up to the main village.)*
For the main walk, turn left and walk beside the stream. Go under the busy road connecting Lausanne and Montreux and, immediately after, under the railway line. This takes you to the shore of **Lake Geneva**. Strolling along the waterfront, you reach a PUBLIC BEACH (**2h50min**); the lawn for sunbathing stretches about 300m up to the **Port de Moratel**.
Follow the quayside to **Cully** (**3h**), an embarkation point for cruises on the lake. The next few minutes are *not* way-marked: at the Hotel Davel opposite the pier, take RUE DAVEL for 100m, to the main road. Cross it and continue along Rue Davel for another 70m, then continue straight ahead along RUE DE LA JUSTICE. After just 50m, turn right. After another 70m or so, take the overpass to cross the main road and the railway line, then turn right. After a few metres you are again on yellow-waymarked territory.
Walk parallel with the railway tracks for 400m, then bear left. Another 400m further on, you come to a narrow path (SENTIER DES BLONNAISSES). This leads you straight through vineyards back to the small community of Epesses, first encountered at the 2h40min-point (**3h20min**).
Now turn left on CHEMIN DE L'OUCHETTE, to the main village of **Epesses**. Turn right and wander along the narrow street

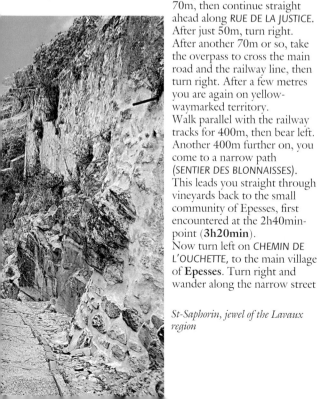

St-Saphorin, jewel of the Lavaux region

through the village for about 120m — to a junction where the Auberge du Vigneron is just 20m ahead. Turn left at this junction, on *CHEMIN DU BOUX* (**3h25min**). This is a very steep road, with a 34% gradient. After a perspiration-inducing ascent, you arrive at a main road in the hamlet of **La Croix** (**3h50min**). Follow this to the right for only 50m, then go right again. You pass a hotel (Le Signal, 649m) and, not far past TENNIS COURTS, leave the surfaced road to take the track to the right. Once on the outskirts of Chexbres, turn left on the road coming from Epesses, cross the railway line, then turn right immediately. After three minutes you arrive at the *RAILWAY STATION* in **Chexbres** (**4h25min**).

The terraced slopes of the Lavaux vineyards are so steep that helicopters are often used to get the grapes out of the vineyards.

Distance/time: The walk is divided into seven sections, which can be done in either direction. (1) Morges — Lausanne-Ouchy: 13km/8mi, 3h; (2) Lausanne-Ouchy — Lutry: 5km/3mi, 1h15min; (3a) Lutry — Cully near the waterfront: 3.5km/2.2mi, 1h or (3b) Lutry — Cully via vineyards: 4.5km/2.8mi, 1h 30min, ascent 180m; (4) Cully — Vevey (via vineyards) 10km/6.2mi, 3h, ascent 250m; (5) Vevey — Montreux: 7.5km/ 4.7mi, 2h; (6) Montreux — Villeneuve 5km/3mi, 1h15min; (7) Villeneuve — Bouveret 8.5km/5.3mi, 2h.

Best period: any time of year
Grade: easy; the terrain is flat except for a mild ascent between Lutry and Cully if the vineyard route (3b) is taken and between Cully and Vevey (another vineyard route). A good part of the walk is along the waterfront, so it should be impossible to get lost!
Equipment: training shoes
Refreshments/accommodation: plenty throughout
Transport: this walk, or parts thereof, is best done one-way and ideally suited for public transport on the return (🚌). The main railway line from Geneva into the Valais stops in Morges, Lausanne (main station), Vevey and Montreux. The S1 urban railway stops at every railway station along the lake from Lausanne to Ville-neuve: Lausanne (main station), Pully, Lutry, Villette, Cully, Epesses, Rivaz, St-Saphorin, Vevey, La Tour-de-Peilz, Burier, Clarens, Montreux, Territet, Veytaux-Chillon, and Villeneuve. The S3 urban railway runs from Lausanne (coming from Allaman) to Villeneuve and stops at Morges, Renens, Lausanne's main station, Pully, Lutry, Cully, Vevey, La Tour-de-Peilz, Clarens, Montreux, and Villeneuve. *Note that* Epesses and Rivaz are up in the hills, but their railway stations are on the shore of the lake. Otherwise, the stations are mostly just a few minutes from the path, or the path passes right by them. To shuttle between Lausanne-Ouchy and Lausanne's main station, take 🚌 18 in front of the railway station to Ouchy (the ter-minus, three stops away). If you are hopping between Vevey, Montreux and Villeneuve, electric city 🚌 1 is very convenient (about every 10min, frequent stops, www. vmcv.ch). Ticket machines are inside the bus. The terminus is Vevey-Funi, from where a 🚡 funicular rises towards Mont Pèlerin (see page 15).

🚗: for the start in Morges take exit 15 (Morges ouest) off the A1 motorway; large parking area near the Parc des sports. There are also car parks in Lausanne-Ouchy, Montreux and Vevey.

Tip: The '**Lavaux Express**', a mini tourist train on tyres (☎ 021 799 54 54, www. lavauxexpress.ch) operates Apr-Oct (from Apr to mid-Jun and in Oct: Wed/Sat/Sun 3-4 times a day; from mid-Jun to end Sep: Wed/Thu/Fri/Sat/ Sun). Departures from Lutry or Cully. Two itineraries: Lutry — Aran — Grandvaux — Lutry (1h); Cully — Riex — Epesses — Dézaley — Cully (1h15min).
Cruising on the lake: boats can be boarded along the coast; see www.cgn.ch.

Some 40km of paths traverse the northern shore of Lake Geneva from Morges past Lausanne, Vevey and Montreux to Bouveret — beautiful walks basking in trees and flowers, interspersed with lovely beaches, restaurants, children's playgrounds, small villages and little ports. But you won't be alone — the vineyards, and mountains rising 2000m above Lake Geneva, give a stunning backdrop, enjoyed by many.

I have split the entire stretch into seven sections, each lasting two to three hours: (1) Morges to Lausanne-Ouchy; (2) Lausanne-Ouchy to Lutry; (3a) Lutry to Cully via vineyards or (3b) near the shore; (4) Cully to Vevey via vineyards; (5) Vevey to Montreux; (6) Montreux to Villeneuve; (7) Villeneuve to Bouveret.

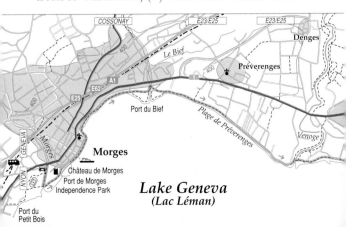

Montreux: flowers in abundance on the Swiss Riviera

1 Morges — Lausanne-Ouchy
From the car park in **Morges**, a town of 14,000 inhabitants, walk alongside the **Morges** stream to the shore of the lake. Cross the bridge and stroll through beautiful **Independence Park**, which explodes with colour during the Tulip Festival from mid-April to mid-May.

You pass the **Port de Morges**, once an important commerical centre, now a yachting harbour. The castle is on your left (**Château de Morges**; open Tue-Fri 10.00-12.00 and 13.30-17.00; Sat/Sun 13.30-17.00; July and August non-stop; closed Mon).

Stroll along the various quays. Go around the **Port du Bief** and pass the beach, **Plage de Préverenges**, to reach the estuary of the **Venoge** stream. Continue to the village of **St-Sulpice**, with its beautiful 13th-century Romanesque church. Follow the village streets AVENUE DE LEMAN, CHEMIN DES PIERRETTES and CHEMIN DU PETIT-PORT to the port at **Les Pierrettes.**

During weekends, you can expect a lot of company on the next stretch — to Ouchy. Take the SENTIER DE LA ROSELIERE to a recreation area and the **Plage de Dorigny**. After crossing another stream, **La Chamberonne**, the **Parc Bourget** is on your left and the **Plage de Vidy** on your right. Continue past Vidy's port to the swimming pool called **Bellerive-Plage**: from October to April, you can continue along the shore, but from May to September you need to circumnavigate the pool via the AVENUE DE RHODANIE. Then follow the quays to the PLACE DE LA NAVIGATION in **Ouchy**.

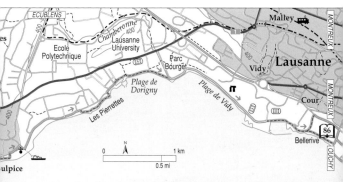

VIDY RAILWAY STATION PRILLY

Pully

Vuachère

Port

Château
d'Ouchy

M

Ouchy

Tour
Haldimand

Chamblandes

Port de Pully

Paudex

0   N   1 km
0.5 mi

Lake Geneva
(Lac Léman)

2 Lausanne-Ouchy — Lutry

In **Ouchy**, strolling along the waterfront, you pass the **Château d'Ouchy**, the elegant hotel Beau-Rivage Palace and the Olympic Museum (Lausanne is the seat of the International Olympic Committee, IOC). When you reach the **Tour Haldimand** (a mock ruin dating from the beginning of the 19th century), cross the **Vuachère** stream, leaving the busy road Quai d'Ouchy behind. Continue on the SENTIER DES RIVES DU LAC, right on the waterfront. You pass a villa which once belonged to General Henri Guisan, Commander-in-Chief of the Swiss Army from 1939-1945.

Harvesting the grapes — and getting them out of the vineyards by monorail (left)

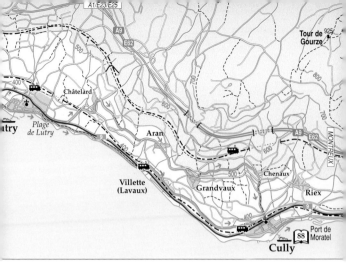

Beyond the village of **Pully**, you come into **Lutry**. Entering Lutry, walk a few metres along the busy road (ROUTE D'OUCHY), but then branch off quickly to the right to follow the quays. After the Quai Gustave Doret and the Quai Vaudère, you reach Lutry's beach (**Plage de Lutry**).

3a Lutry — Cully near the waterfront

From the **Plage de Lutry** continue along the waterfront for about 10 minutes, then use the pavement on the busy road to the railway station at **Villette**. Cross the road via the underpass, turn right and head up gently into the vineyards. The main road and the railway are never far below. When you come to the railway station at **Cully**, make your way (various possibilities) to the PIER.

3b Lutry — Cully via vineyards

This is a slightly more strenuous option, but quieter and more scenic. From the **Plage de Lutry**, take the pedestrian tunnel to the far side of the buzzing Route de Lavaux, then walk 250m southeast towards Vevey. At the HONDA CAR SHOWROOMS take a left up the ROUTE DE LA PETITE CORNICHE. Just after going under the railway bridge, turn right (CHEMIN DU CRET) and reach the hamlet of **Châtelard**. Cross the road, take RUE DU CHATELARD, then turn right on CHEMIN DE CHANTE MERLE, soon crossing a stream. The well-marked route leads you to the village of **Aran**. Follow the CHEMIN DES ECHELETTES and the CHEMIN DES TREIZE VENTS, after which some 200m along the through road brings you into the village of **Grandvaux**. Go downhill on GRAND'RUE, to the centre of the village, and turn left. Cross the road again and go up the SENTIER DES GRANDS JARDINS. Eventually the CHEMIN DE BAUSSAN leads you to the hamlet of **Chenaux**. Here you *leave* the yellow-marked trail: go 100m downhill on the road and on the hairpin bend take the CHEMIN DE CHENAUX straight ahead, which drops off very steeply to **Cully**. Cross the road via the pedestrian overpass and walk through the old town of Cully to reach the PIER.

87

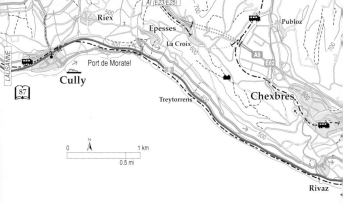

Lake Geneva
(Lac Léman)

4 Cully — Vevey (via vineyards)

From **Cully**, follow Walk 4 (photographs on pages 80-82) in reverse — first alongside the water, then up into the vineyards and through the lower part of **Epesses** and the villages of **Rivaz** and **St-Saphorin**. From St-Saphorin head uphill through the vineyards to the picnic area with the old winepress (see page 80) and, crossing the motorway via an underpass, to the village of **Chardonne**. Now descend to the lake again. A section of yellow-marked path runs steeply downhill alongside the Vevey–Mont Pèlerin funicular (you could hop on that). After **Corseaux** follow the CHEMIN DE BASSET to the NESTLÉ HEADQUARTERS in **Vevey** and from there walk along the lake to the GRANDE-PLACE.

The Castle of Chillon, with the Dents du Midi behind the lake

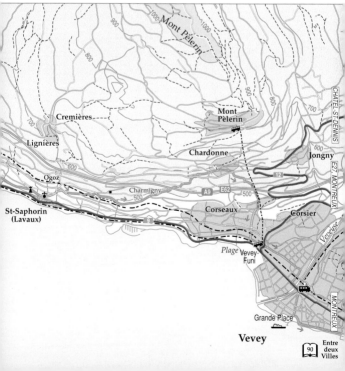

5 Vevey — Montreux

From the *GRANDE-PLACE* in **Vevey** (see map on page 89), follow the beautiful waterfront, passing the statue of Charlie Chaplin and the Museum of Nutrition to reach the town **La Tour-de-Peilz**. Round the *CASTLE* which hosts the Swiss Toy Museum (Musée Suisse du Jeu) and walk along to the *PORT*.

When you reach the beach of **La Becque**, the waterfront walk unfortunately comes to an end for the time being. You now need to follow a rather noisy road for 2km —interrupted by the beautiful **Plage de la Maladaire**. (As an alternative, you can simply take a frequent electric city bus 1 from La Becque's bus stop to the Basset bus stop at the entrance to **Clarens**, from where you fork right to the port at Clarens.) Then either walk on to the railway station or continue to Montreux along a splendid lakeshore path.

6 Montreux — Villeneuve

You can't get lost on the path from **Clarens** via Montreux to Villeneuve: simply follow the magnificent shoreline and enjoy the exuberant vegetation — with a great variety of trees, shrubs and flowers, and breathtaking views to the Swiss and French Alps on the far side of Lake Geneva. No wonder that this region, the **Swiss Riviera**, seduced a large number of artists: Rousseau, Byron, Bocion, Hugo, James, Dostoievsky, Stravinsky, Haskil, Hemingway, and Nabokov among them.

Montreux is a bustling place, and world-famous for its Jazz Festival. Passing the towns of **Trex**, **Bon Port** and **Territet**, you reach the most beautifully situated castle in Switzerland — the **Château de Chillon**

Chailly

Les Avants

Chernex

Vuarennes

A9

Clarens

E62

de

Montreux

Vaunaises

Vernex

Les Planches

Baye

Glion

Caux

Montreux

Trex

Bon Port

La Veraye

Lake Geneva
(Lac Léman)

Territet

Veytaux

(open daily, www.chillon.ch).
It is one of the best-preserved
medieval castles in Europe,
immortalized in Byron's 1816
poem *The Prisoner of Chillon*.
Continue along the waterfront
to the town **Villeneuve**.

Château
de Chillon

7 Villeneuve — Bouveret
From **Villeneuve**, you can
continue following the yellow-
waymarked and signposted
route through the natural
reserve **Les Grangettes** and
along the **Rhône** estuary to the
hamlet of **Bouveret**.

Grandchamp

La Tinière

A9

Villeneuve

E62

Les Grangettes

Eau Froide

Noville

BOUVERET

MARTIGNY

Distance/time: 3km/2mi; 1h40min

Best period: June until October

Grade: a short but challenging walk; you must be sure-footed and have a head for heights to tackle the ladders and switch-back paths. Ascent 360m/1200ft, descent 120m/400ft; highest point 2042m, lowest 1700m

Equipment: hiking boots; torch and warm clothing if you climb through the Grottes de Naye

Refreshments/accommodation: refreshments at Jaman railway station on the mountain. Restaurant-Hotel Plein Roc on top of the mountain (dormitories; panoramic restaurant; (021 963 74 11) — accessed via a 220m-long tunnel from the Rochers de Naye terminus station. Plenty of rooms in Montreux.

Transport: 🚆 from platform 8 at Montreux's railway station to Rochers de Naye; hourly. Alight at Jaman station (some 1300m above Montreux) — the third to last station on the line, journey time 46min. Note that in summer, the last train from Rochers de Naye down to Montreux leaves before 19.00.

Shorter walks

1 Rochers de Naye: stroll around the summit and botanical garden (distance/time optional). The train ride up to Rochers de Naye takes 55min. The vista from the VIEWING PLATFORM is a 10-minute walk from the terminus. In the other direction, it is a 15-minute stroll to the Alpine garden **La Ramberta** (founded in

1896), to admire some thousand species.

2 Dent de Jaman (50min, ascent 140m; you must be sure-footed and have a head for heights). This grassy 'sugar loaf' peak (1875m) just north of Jaman station can be crested on a narrow footpath; it's just 30min up and 20min down — and there is a great view (see photograph pages 94-95).

Alternative walks

1 Rochers de Naye circuit from Jaman station (3h25min, ascent 500m, more demanding than the main walk; *one potentially dangerous stretch*). Follow the main walk to **Rochers de Naye** (1h 40min). To return, descend towards SAUTADOZ from the signpost 'jungle' close to the restaurant. When you reach the **Sautodoz** saddle (1832m, 15min from the restaurant), turn right. A few minutes later

you're descending a very steep slope full of scree. Take care not to loosen any stones, and watch out for people above you. (A sign in French warns that this is a dangerous trail.) After about 15min this section is behind you. At the next junction (1680m), bear right and start the moderate climb to **La Perche** (1799m), the penultimate station on the line. Then walk down the *cirque* (1700m) and up to **Jaman** station (1739m).

2 Caux — Rochers de Naye (5h25min, ascent 900m, more demanding than the main walk; *one potentially dangerous stretch*). 🚃 take the train from Montreux towards Rochers de Naye, but get off at **Haut-de-Caux** station (1160m) — 33min from Montreux and the second station after Caux; 🚗 there is a parking area here as well. Walk along the surfaced road which passes under the railway line. At the signposted junction **Liboson d'en Haut** (1275m, 30min) follow the sign for *LA PERCHE*. The path meanders up to a junction at 1631m (1h40min). Bear right here, and go right again at the next the junction. Now you have to tackle a very steep scree slope. Take care not to loosen any stones, and watch out for people above you — this is a potentially dangerous stretch. Once on the **Sautodoz** saddle (1838m, 2h20min), follow the signposting to **Rochers de Naye** (3h). After a break, retrace your steps to the **Sautodoz** saddle (3h25min) and leave it on the path to the left. This path loses altitude gently and is very pleasant. At the junction 1420m (*SIGNPOST*, 4h30min), turn right and follow a woodland road back via **Liboson d'en Haut** (5h05min) to **Haut-de-Caux** (5h25min).

Rochers de Naye as seen from the Dent de Jaman (Short walk 2), with the railway meandering through tunnels to the top. Below right: the fixed ladders leading up to the ridge

(3) Col de Jaman — Rochers de Naye (5h, ascent 630m, more demanding than the main walk; *one potentially dangerous stretch*). Access by 🚗: drive from Montreux up to the parking area at Col de Jaman (1522m) — either via Les Avants or via Caux (both are narrow roads). Following signposting to the JAMAN railway station, *descend* the valley in a south-easterly direction (1477m), then continue straight ahead and climb the same path to 1703m (SIGNPOST, 1h). Pick up the main walk here, and follow it from the 10min-point to the end (2h20min). Then use the notes for Alternative walk 1 on page 92 from **Rochers de Naye** to **Jaman** station (4h15min). From Jaman station (1739m) follow signposting (COL DE JAMAN) towards the Dent de Jaman, but after five minutes make a U-bend to the left, to go south again. Ten minutes later make another 180° bend, this time to the right. Follow the western flank of the **Dent de Jaman** back to the **Col de Jaman** (5h).

R ochers de Naye (2045m) is Montreux's mountain. The circuit described is marvellous, starting with a spectacular train ride from Montreux on the shores of Lake Geneva up the Rochers de Naye, continuing with a short but demanding walk, and culminating with a feast for the eyes from the summit — looking down over the lake and across to the Swiss and French Alps as well as the Jura.

From **Jaman** station (1739m), cross the railway tracks and take the signposted (COL DE BONAUDON) path down to the *cirque*. At 1703m (**10min**) again follow COL DE BONAUDON and start climbing. At the junction on the **Col de Bonaudon** (1755m, **25min**), bear right towards ROCHERS DE NAYE and descend a bit, through an area littered with boulders. You arrive at a rock wall with fixed ladders; the entrance to the **Grottes de Naye** is just a few metres away (**30min**). Two challenging alternatives confront you now.

If you are not claustrophobic, have brought a torch and warm clothing — and *if there is no snow which might block the exit* (after mid-July), you may want to climb up through the Grottes de Naye. This takes about 15 minutes, gaining 50m in height. Inside the grotto you *must always bear left* (a sign in French at the entrance emphasizes it) — so about midway after the ladders do *not* go towards a small window of daylight, but keep left. At the beginning the opening is so narrow that you have to crawl through. You will encounter ladders and handrails. Take care: the floor of the caves is slippery. Once you get up to the exit, pick up the text below after the ladders.

The second option is to climb up the somewhat vertiginous

ladders and steps secured to the rock, then follow a few switch-backs on the steep slope, up to the ridge (1850m, **45min**). From the ridge you see the railway terminus and the transmitter tower on the summit of the Rochers de Naye.

Walk along the grassy ridge to the top of the **Rochers de Naye** (**1h30min**). From the railway station (1970m, **1h40min**) take the train back to Montreux.

Walk 7 (Jura): LA DOLE

Distance/time: 12km/7.5mi; 4h30min

Best period: May/June to October/November — or a great winter walk on snow-shoes, very popular on sunny days

Grade: moderate-strenuous, with an ascent of 650m/2130ft; highest point 1677m, lowest 1150m

Equipment: hiking boots

Refreshments/accommodation: La Givrine railway stop, Couvaloup de Crans; nearest accommodation in St-Cergue

Transport: 🚆 to Nyon (Geneva–Lausanne line, frequent departures), then 🚆 to La Givrine (Nyon–La Cure line, hourly every day, journey time about 45min). 🚗 exit 11

for Nyon off the A1 motorway between Geneva and Lausanne, then head to St-Cergue. In St-Cergue go left towards La Cure, stopping at the railway station at La Givrine (parking alongside the road, also car park).

Shorter walks

1 La Dôle out and back (3h 50min, 500m ascent). Walk back the way you came.

2 La Dôle from the Chalet de la Dôle (1h30min, ascent 250m, easy). 🚗 as above: take the road towards St-Cergue, but go left at the second roundabout. Go through Gingins and rise in hairpins to the Chalet de la Dôle (1439m), starting point of a signposted circuit via La Dôle.

W hether you come to Geneva by plane or travel on the motorway from Lausanne, a big white globe on the Jura mountain range will grab your attention. It's the aerial navigation system for Geneva airport, and it sits on top of La Dôle — the second-highest mountain in the Swiss Jura at 1677m.

At the small RAILWAY STOP of **La Givrine** (1208m), cross the road and go through the turn-stile. Take the path that runs diagonally across a meadow. After 400m/5min you reach the FIRST SIGNPOST (**5min**). Bear right towards LA DOLE and walk alongside the stone wall. After 200m continue on a dirt road which, after another 200m, bends left (**10min**). Pass the signpost '**La Trélasse**' (1199m, **12min**) and continue on the road until you are about 100m from the lower station of a small SKI LIFT (**40min**).

View towards La Dôle, where the navigation system for Geneva's airport is visible to the left; note the typical yellow rhombus waymark.

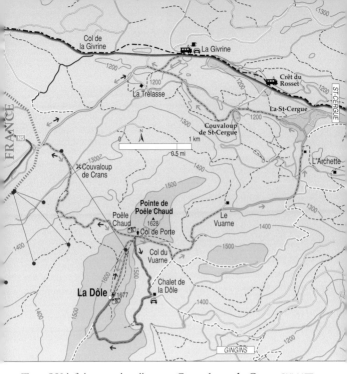

Turn 90° left here and walk up the hill. After some 100m, you pass through a gap in the wall (*YELLOW RHOMBUS*). When you reach the valley station of the

Couvaloup de Crans *SKI LIFT*, climb up parallel with the lift for 300m. Then, at the edge of the woods, follow the trail to the right, moving away from

Mont Blanc from La Dôle

the ski lift (**55min**) and now following the SKI RUN. After 15 minutes you pass a neon(!) sign for the 'Cuvaloup' Restaurant (**1h10min**) on the right-hand side of the ski run (the more common spelling is Couvaloup). The path turns left and follows the edge of the woods.

When you see the white globe again (**1h25min**), one possibility is to head straight towards it. However, the waymarked trail actually goes left, turning away from the globe and losing a little height. When you have passed through another stone wall, you see a building about 200m in front of you. Head towards it and cross the ski lift just there (**Poêle Chaud**, 1465m, **1h40min**). The trail leaves the ski lift behind and rises to the **Col de Porte** (1557m, **2h**), with a view over Lake Geneva and to the Alps. Turn right and, walking on the ridge, head to the top of **La Dôle** (1677m, **2h20min**).

Return to the **Col de Porte** (**2h35min**). Three trails go down to the right from this pass. Take the middle one — the one that slopes down just before the SKI HUT. It bends

98

right and comes to an intersection (signpost **Col du Vuarne**, 1470m, **2h45min**). Turn left, pass through another stone wall after 100m, and follow the signs as the trail goes down more steeply than it has up until now, describing a curve to the left.

At the SIGNPOST **Le Vuarne** (1319m, **3h10min**) the path becomes a surfaced road. Pass a SIGNPOST, **Route du Vuarne** (1269m, **3h25min**) and, two minutes later, leave the road: take the path to the left, signposted to L'ARCHETTE, heading across meadows. At a CABIN (parking area and SIGNPOST **L'Archette**, 1162m, **3h37min**) you're back on the road. You pass the SIGNPOST **La St-Cergue** (1150m, **3h40min**); two minutes later, turn left uphill through a residential area (CHEMIN DES GENTIANES).

At the end of the road, take the trail that goes downhill through the woods. At the SIGNPOST **Couvaloup de St-Cergue** (1196m, **4h**), turn left on a surfaced road but, after 50m, bear right and follow the signposted path across undulating meadows. Cross a surfaced road (**4h15min**) and shortly thereafter reach a stone wall which you follow for just a minute — to arrive back at the FIRST SIGNPOST that you passed at the 5min-point in the walk. Turn sharply right, and you will be back at the **La Givrine** RAILWAY STOP (**4h30min**).

Walk 8 (Jura): MONT TENDRE

Distance/time: 16km/10mi; 5h15min

Best period: May-October

Grade: moderate-strenuous, but technically easy. Ascent 650m/2130ft; highest point 1679m, lowest 1447m

Equipment: hiking boots

Refreshments/accommodation: hotel/restaurant at the Col du Marchairuz (rooms and dormitories), (021 845 25 30, www.hotel-marchairuz.ch;

refreshments available at the Chalet du Mont Tendre (1615m), 15min on foot from the north side of the summit

Transport: 🚐 from Nyon (on the busy Geneva–Lausanne railway line) to the Col du Marchairuz (runs twice a day, morning and afternoon, between Jun-Sep, *but only on weekends and on 1 Aug, the Swiss National Holiday*), journey time 1h; or 🚐 from Le Brassus

Cow with headdress on one of Mont Tendre's meadows

(twice a day, around 10.00 and 16.00, between Jun-Sep, *but only on weekends*, journey time 18min). 🚗: exit 12 (Gland) from the A1 Geneva–Lausanne motorway, then drive via Begnins and Burtigny to the parking area at the Col du Marchairuz.

Short walk: stroll to Mont Tendre (15min, easy). 🚗: exit 14 (Aubonne) off the A1 motorway and drive via Ballens and Mollens to Montricher. From Montricher a narrow road snakes up to the parking area at the Chalet du Mont Tendre. It's just a 15-minute ramble to the summit.

Alternative walks
1 Mont Tendre from the Lac de Joux (grade as main walk, with an ascent of 800m and descent of 350m, 5h45min; *you will need a map*). From the village Le Pont at the north-eastern end of Lake Joux (🚗: see Car tour 2), follow sign-posting/waymarks to Mont Tendre via the Chalet du Mont Tendre, then do the main walk to the Col du Marchairuz. Return by 🚌 to Le Brassus and Le Pont.

2 Circuit from Montricher (strenuous, with an ascent of 1050m, 6h15min; *you will need a map*). Access by 🚌 from Morges to Montricher (Morges–L'Isle line, see page 57, runs every 1-2h, journey time 25min); change trains in Apples. 🚗: exit 14 (Aubonne) off the A1 motorway and drive

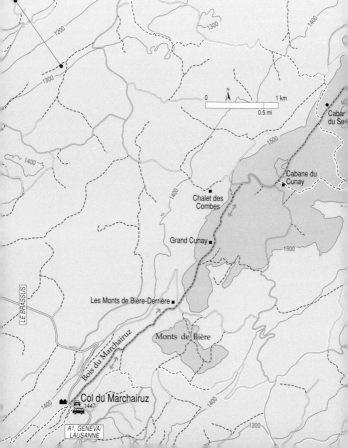

via Ballens and Mollens to Montricher. There is a parking area on the outskirts of the forest west of Montricher. Walk north through forest and up Mont Châtel (1432m, great view), then descend 150m in height and climb Mont Tendre heading southwest from the Chalet du Mont Tendre. Return to the chalet and walk via the Chalet Neuf du Mont Tendre and Pré Anselme back to Montricher.

M ont Tendre, at 1679m, is the highest peak in the Swiss Jura and also the point from which you can see the entire shoreline of Lake Geneva spread below you. In winter this is a popular snowshoe route. The undulating trail leads in an almost straight line north-east to the summit.

The signposted and way-marked trail starts on the **Col du Marchairuz** (1447m), opposite the hotel. You first walk through forest to the chalet **Les Monts de Bière-Derrière** (1481m, **35min**).

Just behind the **Grand Cunay** barn (1567m, **1h**) the trail bears left and descends slightly. Meeting a surfaced road (1518m, **1h15min**), follow it uphill for about 600m, then fork left, back on the trail. After 100m you see the **Cabane du Cunay** about 100m to your right. Continue straight on. Past the **Cabane du Servan** (1555m, **1h55min**) and the **Chalet de Yens** (1589m, **2h05min**), you tackle the final ascent to the summit of **Mont Tendre** (1679m, **2h30min**).
A hearty meal can be had if you follow the path along the ridge downhill for about 800m (15 minutes) to the **Chalet du Mont Tendre** (1615m, **2h45min**).
Retrace your steps to the **Col du Marchairuz** (**5h15min**).

Winter trails in the Jura

Walk 9 (Jura): POËTA RAISSE GORGE AND LE CHASSERON

Distance/time: 22km/13.6mi; 6h15min
Best period: May until November. The gorge is particularly impressive on a rainy day, when the water forces its way down — but then you have take special care on the slippery boardwalks.

The gorge is *dangerous* when there is ice or snow.
Grade: strenuous, with an ascent of 870m/2850ft (highest point 1607m, lowest 739m). You may need to have a head for heights, but the path and steps through the gorge are secured with handrails.

An exciting part of the trail through the Poëta Raisse Gorge

Equipment: hiking boots
Refreshments/accommodations: Hôtel du Chasseron just below the summit, open throughout the year except Mondays; rooms and dormitories (024 454 23 88, www.chasseron.ch. Refreshments at Les Preisettes.
Transport: 🚌 to Môtiers (Neuchâtel–Fleurier–Buttes line, usually every hour from Neuchâtel). From the railway station in Môtiers (735m) it is about 100m to the main street (Rue Centrale; the arched building here, the Hôtel des Six Communes, has a restaurant). Cross over Rue Centrale and follow the wide Grande Rue (with fountain and post office) out of the village for 1.1km, to the parking area in the forest, where the walk starts (20min). 🚗: drive from Neuchâtel or Ste-Croix to Môtiers, then fork off in the centre of the village on Grande Rue; this leads to a parking area in the woods, where the walk starts.

Shorter walks
1 Poëta Raisse Gorge (2h 45min, grade as main walk, but ascent of 380m). Go through the gorge to the signpost 1131m and return the same way.
2 Château de Môtiers (2h 10min, easy-moderate, with an ascent of 300m overall). From the parking area follow the main walk to the junction at 1008m. Take a sharp right here. Descend and pass close to a farm (Le Breuil), after which there's a small gain in height of 40m. Go about 100m downhill on the forest road and continue straight ahead on the hairpin bend, on a lovely woodland track to the castle (Château de Môtiers). Then walk on to the

railway station at Môtiers or back to the parking area.
3 Poëta Raisse and high plain, omitting Chasseron (4h40min, grade as main walk, but ascent of 670m). Follow the main walk to the farm Les Cernets Dessus (1406m) and continue on the gravel road for 400m, then branch off right to Les Preisettes. Pick up the main walk again at the 4h25min-point.
Alternative walks (*not all shown on the map overleaf; you will need a map*)
1 Le Chasseron from Les Rasses (2h, easy-moderate, ascent 410m). See Car tour 3, and drive from Ste-Croix to Les Rasses, from where you can follow signposts up to the summit of Chasseron in 1h 15min. Return the same way. You can shorten this walk even further by driving past Les Rasses, up to 1440m — from there it's only 20min to the summit.
2 Ste-Croix — Le Chasseron — Môtiers (4h45min, ascent 520m, descent 870m, moderate, access by 🚌). This linear walk starts in Ste-Croix. From the railway station, a well-marked path leads in 2h to the summit of Le Chasseron. Once there, pick up the main walk at the 3h35min-point and follow it to the end. To get back to your starting point at Ste-Croix from Môtiers, take the local 🚌 to Buttes (hourly). From Buttes there is a 🚌 to Ste-Croix (2-3 times a day; journey time 30min). Alternatively, take the long route by train from Môtiers — via Neuchâtel and Yverdon-les-Bains to Ste-Croix (journey time 2h20min).

This walk features two highlights: the Poëta Raisse Gorge and Mount Chasseron. Poëta Raisse is one of the most impressive gorges in the Jura. Boardwalks and footbridges, secured with handrails, allow hikers to traverse this deep chasm with its small waterfalls. Chasseron, at 1607m, shares the honour of being the third-highest summit in the Swiss Jura with similar-sounding Chasseral (Walk 11). Both offer splendid views of the entire Alpine chain.

From the PARKING AREA in the forest at **Môtiers** (757m) follow the stream (**Ruisseau du Breuil**), which will be your companion for 1h30min or so and which you will cross a couple of times. The broad gravel path at first slopes gently uphill, then narrows and becomes more steep. You eventually come to a junction (SIGNPOST: 1008m, **45min**). *(Shorter walk 2 turns sharp right here.)*
Some 50m after the junction cross the stream (*don't go straight ahead*). The first of the two exciting sections of the **Poëta Raisse Gorge** is about to start. Steps hewn from the rock and boardwalks with handrails lead through this part. After this steep passage, continue straight ahead (*don't go left across the bridge*). You reach another junction (SIGNPOST: 1065m, **1h05min**) where you ignore a path off right to Fleurier. Shortly after, tackle the second exciting part of the gorge — slightly more challenging than the first part (there is a steep drop of some 5m, but a handrail helps). When you reach SIGNPOST 1131m (**1h30min**; picnic area), the gorge is behind you. *(Shorter walk 1 turns back here.)*
Go straight on and come to a pasture with a farm (**La Vaux**) about 100m up the hillside. Don't take the trail which kinks

almost 180° to the right, but continue straight ahead across the pasture. The path bends slightly to the right, enters forest again and meets a gravel road. Bear right. After less than 10 minutes on the gravel road, leave it and head straight on, following a narrow trail which runs parallel with electricity poles (**2h05min**).
Coming to another mountain pasture, you pass by a farm (**Les Cernets Dessus**, 1406m, **2h30min**). Follow the gravel road from here and, 400m past the farm, ignore a trail branching off right to Les Preisettes. *(But take this trail if*

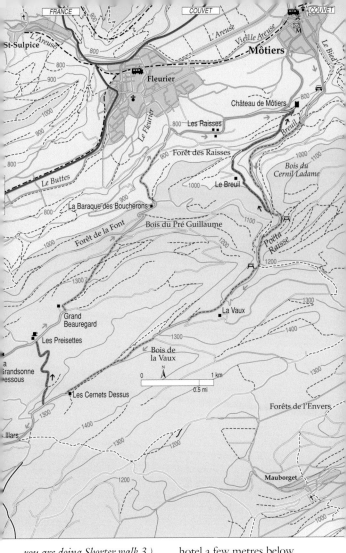

you are doing Shorter walk 3.)
Continue on the gravel road
which bends left and meets a
surfaced road. Follow this
uphill and, at a junction
(*SIGNPOST: Les Illars*, 1427m,
2h45min) bear right on
another road. Fifteen minutes
later, leave the road for
mountain pastures (*SIGNPOST*,
3h). Follow the faint but
waymarked path up to the
summit of **Le Chasseron**
(1607m, **3h35min**) and the

hotel a few metres below.
Retrace your steps until you
get to the signposted junction
at 1552m (**3h45min**) but now
bear left, crossing pastures on a
beautiful trail. At the next
junction (**4h**), ignore the path
which descends left through
forest to Ste-Croix, as well as
the path signposted 'Fleurier
2h10min'; instead, bear right
(signposted *FLEURIER 2h*).
This path meets a surfaced
road (**4h10min**), which you

View from Le Chasseron

follow straight ahead, passing various farms — first **La Grandsonne Dessous** (1338m), then **Les Preisettes** (1328m, **4h25min**, refreshments available; *Shorter walk 3 comes in here*), and finally **Grand Beauregard** (1332m, **4h35min**).

During the next 10 minutes pay particular attention to the signposts and waymarks. A few metres past the Beauregard farm, *leave* the road and bend left across pastures, to enter the forest (**4h45min**). The trail cuts across various forestry roads, then follows one of these roads for a couple of hairpin bends, passing a new log cabin (**La Baraque des Bucherons, 5h05min**). Be sure, past this cabin (after the curve), to rejoin the trail by

kinking right (SIGNPOST). You catch glimpses of Fleurier through the forest.

You leave the forest at a signposted junction (808m, **5h 20min**), by turning right and following a surfaced road uphill for a few metres before turning left towards MOTIERS. Go through **Les Raisses**, a hamlet of just three houses. Following the signs (left, then right), you pass about 100m to the left of the **Château de Môtiers**, somewhat hidden in the forest. The road descends to **Môtiers** and merges with the GRANDE RUE (**6h05min**; small museum devoted to Jean-Jacques Rousseau). Turn left at this junction to return to the railway station, or turn right, to walk back to the PARKING AREA in the forest (**6h15min**).

Walk 10 (Jura): AREUSE GORGE, CREUX DU VAN AND LE SOLIAT

See also photographs on pages 4 and 22
Distance/time: 18km/11.2mi; 6h05min
Best period: May to October
Grade: moderate-strenuous, with a steep ascent from La Fontaine Froide up to the top of the Creux du Van. All on good trails; overall ascent 850m/2790ft; highest point 1465m, lowest 615m
Equipment: hiking boots
Refreshments/accommodation: La Ferme Robert, accommodation must be booked several weeks in advance, ✆ 032 863 31 40, www.ferme-robert. ch; La Ferme du Soliat, dormitory (60 places), ✆ 032 863 31 36, www.pellaux.ch/soliat. html; Les Oeuillons (refreshments only), ✆ 032 863 31 35; L'Auberge de Noiraigue, rooms and dormitories, cl Wed, ✆ 032 863 37 06; Restaurant La Truite in Champ du Moulin, 200m from the Maison de la Nature across the stream, ✆ 032 855 11 34.
Transport: 🚂 to Champ du Moulin (Neuchâtel–Fleurier–Buttes line, hourly departures from Neuchâtel). From the railway station walk down the road for 7min to the Maison de la Nature. 🚗: from the road between Neuchâtel and Fleurier, fork south between Brot-Dessous and Rochefort towards Champ du Moulin and follow this narrow surfaced road for 3km, down to the bottom of the valley; two-thirds of the way down you pass the isolated Champ du Moulin railway station. Once in the valley, do not cross the bridge, but drive about 100m further, to the Maison de la Nature (small museum),

and park in the meadow just behind the building.
Shorter walks
1 Creux du Van from Ferme Robert (3h20min, grade as main walk, but ascent of 570m). Access by 🚗: from Noiraigue, drive up to La Ferme Robert (972m) and park there. Follow the main walk from the 1h35min-point to the 4h25min-point, then head back to Ferme Robert.
2 Areuse Gorge (just over 1h *each way*, easy, access by 🚂 or 🚗. Follow the main walk to Saut de Brot and continue straight on to Noiraigue, then retrace your steps (or vice-versa). Or just do as a linear walk and take the train back.
3 Creux du Van in 10min. In the village of Couvet in the Val de Travers (Car tour 3) a road branches off to the Ferme du Soliat. From there it's just a few minutes to the *cirque*.

Romantic humpback bridge spanning the Areuse River in the eponymous gorge

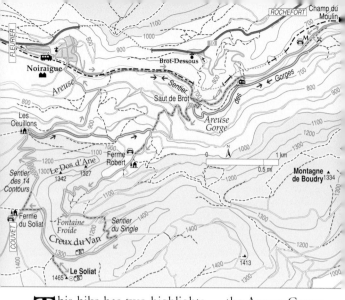

This hike has two highlights — the Areuse Gorge, where a Venetian-like bridge spans the sometimes-wild Areuse River, and the Creux du Van *cirque*, perhaps the most popular goal for hikers in the Swiss Jura.

The **Maison de la Nature** at **Champ du Moulin** (615m) is a small museum of Neuchâtel's natural history (open weekends from mid-May to end Sep, 10.00-17.00, entry free). From the building take the way-marked paved track to a

HYDROELECTRIC PLANT (**15min**). Here the track eventually becomes a footpath and enters the **Areuse Gorge**. Before long you cross the **Areuse River** on the picturesque bridge shown on page 107 (**35min**), where the gorge is at its narrowest point. A couple of minutes later, turn left at a junction (SIGNPOST: **Saut de Brot**, 651m) and a few metres further on, bear right on the signposted and waymarked path.

This forest path snakes up to the Ferme Robert, crossing forest roads and the access road to Ferme Robert a few times. **Ferme Robert** (972m, **1h 35min**) is an old farmhouse, now a restaurant with accommodation. A few metres behind it, keep straight on and rise to the **Fontaine Froide** ('Cold Fountain', 1126m, **2h10min**). Ignore the forest path that turns right 60m past the fountain but keep ahead and, three minutes later, turn right at a junction. This path (**Sentier du Single**) is *steep*. Arriving at a T-junction (SIGNPOST: 1414m, **3h**), go right; five minutes later you are at the edge of the **Creux du Van**.

Now just walk along the edge of the crater, but add two small detours: from halfway round (**3h15min**) you can reach the peak of **Soliat** (1465m, ORIENTATION TABLE) in five minutes — with a splendid view of the Alps. Then, almost all the way round (**3h35min**), it's just another five-minute walk to the **Ferme du Soliat** (1382m, refreshments).

Return from here to the edge of the crater (**3h45min**). After a few minutes, the trail veers away from the *cirque* and zigzags comfortably down the steep slope through 14 hairpin bends (**Sentier des 14 Contours**) to a farm, **Les Oeuillons** (1014m, refreshments; **4h25min**). *(For Shorter walk 1, follow signposting and waymarks from here back to Ferme Robert.)*

Behind the Oeuillons farm the main walk towards NOIRAIGUE turns sharply right, then descends less steeply. In **Noiraigue** (728m, **5h05min**), turn right immediately after crossing the railway line; you cross the railway line again after about five minutes. From now on you will follow the powerful Areuse River back to the parking area. Cross the river shortly before the **Saut de Brot** junction (651m, **5h35min**), and retrace your steps to the **Maison de la Nature** (**6h05min**).

Creux du Van

Walk 11 (Jura): COMBE GRÈDE AND LE CHASSERAL

Distance/time: 18km/11.2mi; 6h15min

Best period: May/June until October/November

Grade: strenuous; you must be sure-footed and have a head for heights when zigzagging up the Combe Grède (handrails help); three ladders; watch out for falling rocks. Ascent about 1000m/3300ft; highest point 1607m, lowest 757m

Equipment: hiking boots

Refreshments/accommodation: quite large hotel/restaurant on the ridge of Chasseral (1548m), with rooms and dormitories, (032 751 24 51, www.chasseral-hotel.ch. The hotel can re reached by car and public transport. Refreshments at the Métairie des Plânes; accommodation in St-Imier

Transport: 🚌 either from Neuchâtel to La Chaux-de-Fonds (changing for St-Imier, hourly, journey 44min), or from Biel/Bienne to St-Imier (twice an hour, journey time 26min or 39min, depending on the train). 🚗: drive from Neuchâtel or Biel/Bienne to St-Imier. There is also a *narrow road* up to the Hôtel Chasseral — the junction is about 5km before St-Imier when coming from Neuchâtel.

Shorter walks

1 Descent from Chasseral (2h20min, fairly easy descent of about 850m). From Jun-Oct, a 🚌 runs from St-Imier's railway station to the Hôtel Chasseral (3 times/day, journey time 36min). Ride up and follow the main walk from the 3h55min-point.

2 Ridge walk (time immaterial, easy). 🚗 *(narrow road)* or 🚌 (as above) to the Hôtel Chasseral; walk along the ridge for as long as you like.

3 Villeret to Chasseral (about 5h via the direct route from Pré aux Auges to the Chasseral Hotel, grade as main walk).

Villeret is a village adjacent to St-Imier. 🚆: trains every hour from Biel/Bienne to Villeret (*note:* not all trains to St-Imier stop in Villeret); then walk to the parking area for motorists (15min). 🚗: from the main street in Villeret, a road signposted to Combe Grède forks south for 600m to a parking/picnic area (767m). Whether you come by car or on foot, walk 100m from the parking area, then bear right to reach the main walk route after further 10min. Pick up the main walk notes between the 30min- and 1h-points. On the return, at the 5h10min-point

(L'Ilsach *signpost*), turn right to the Combe Grède signpost (911m) and from there retrace your steps to the parking area. **4 Villeret — Combe Grède** (2h15min, moderate, with an ascent of 400m, access as Shorter walk 3). Follow Shorter walk 3 to the 1h-point in the main walk (Combe Grède junction; 911m), then bear *right,* quickly coming to L'Ilsach. Pick up the main walk here (at the 5h10min-point) and follow it to the junction 200m before the Bénonne farm, then turn right and walk back to Villeret via the Métairie au Renard farm.

After a taxing ascent through the Combe Grède, a gash-like cleft in the mountains, you have sweeping 360° views from the summit of Chasseral — encompassing three lakes — Neuchâtel, Biel and Morat. Except for birds and the occasional burbling of water, total silence reigns in the Combe Grède fissure — a total contrast to Chasseral's accessible and busy summit!

Take the underpass at the railway station in **St-Imier** (795m) and descend to the Longines watchmaking plant. Go round the building following signposting. The way-marked route heads towards the edge of the forest. Some 15 minutes from setting out, when the dirt road curves to the right, continue *straight ahead* and follow the path alongside the trees (YELLOW RHOMBUS WAYMARK on a tree a bit further ahead). You then walk through a military shooting range (during practice, a well-marked detour shown in lilac on the map, *deviation en cas de tir,* skirts this area). When the track meets a surfaced road (**30min**), follow

Meadow past the farm La Bénnone (near the end of the walk)

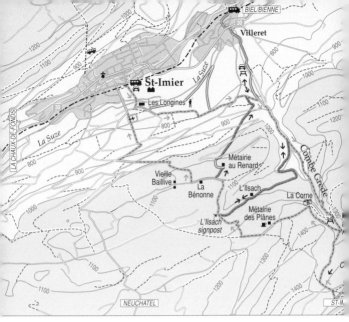

this to the left for 60m, then fork right, into the forest. A couple of minutes later bear left at the junction, and three minutes later meet a track which comes up from the village of Villeret. *(Shorter walks 3 and 4 come in here.)*

The second and third ladders in the Combe Grède are adjacent.

At the SIGNPOST **Combe Grède** (911m, **1h**) bear left. The first LADDER encountered (**1h25min**) has only 11 steps, but five minutes later two adjacent ladders (11 steps, then 30 steps; see photograph) are more demanding. Then the steep trail snakes its way up the fissure.

Once you have reached the **Pré aux Auges**, signalled by a FIRST SIGNPOST (1267m, picnic area/fireplace, **2h10min**) and a SECOND SIGNPOST five minutes later (1277m), the most challenging part of the walk is behind you. You now have two choices for the ascent.

The main walk heads quite gently up the grassy valley on the left to a dairy farm, the **Chalet Métairie de Morat** (1465m, **3h**) and from there up to **Chasseral** (1607m, **3h35min**) with its huge TV/radio tower. This is the third-highest mountain in the Swiss Jura, but shares that distinction with the similar-sounding Chasseron (Walk 9). From the summit, walk on to

The long, almost-level Chasseral ridge is perfect for a short walk; the summit itself is marked by a monstrous TV tower.

the HOTEL (1548m, **3h55min**). For a shorter, but steeper approach, bear *right* from the SECOND SIGNPOST at the Pré aux Auges. In this case you will reach the hotel first — saving almost an hour — and you are not missing much by skipping Chasseral's summit. The main walk uses this trail for the *descent*.

For the return, walk 150m from the hotel towards the TV tower, then take a trail which descends to the left (signpost: CHEMIN DES CRETES). Cross the road twice and descend in a right-hand curve into the valley to come back to the SIGNPOST 1277m at **Pré aux Auges** (**4h25min**) — this is the same trail used for the shorter ascent mentioned above.

Turn 90° left at this junction and follow the gently-rising forestry trail. When you leave the forest, be sure to take a detour a few metres to the right off the path — to an impressive cliff-edge viewpoint with handrail (**La Corne**, 1333m, **4h40min**), from where you look out over St-Imier and the Combe Grède.

Pass another dairy farm, the **Métairie des Plânes** (1289m, refreshments, **4h50min**), and continue ahead for another 200m. Then take the trail forking off to the right. This crosses meadows and comes to a junction (**5h**). Both forks lead back to St-Imier (and take about the same time). But take the fork to the right, descending more steeply through forest. When you reach a gravel path, follow it to the left (SIGNPOST: **L'Ilsach**, 1110m, **5h10min**). (*But for Shorter walk 3 turn right here.*) The path rises very slightly. At the next junction, turn left and, 100m further on, at the following junction, continue straight ahead. When you pass a farm (**La Bénonne**; **5h25min**) you only have another 130m to go on the surfaced road, then turn 90° to the right (SIGNPOST) and cross a meadow. After 150m the trail turns left for 170m, then zigzags right and left (SIGNS mark this zigzag, but you have to watch out for them). Continue through forest back to **St-Imier** (**6h15min**).

113

Walk 12 (Jura): MOUNT WEISSENSTEIN

Distance/time: 13.5km/ 8.4mi; 4h50min. Allow an hour extra for a detour to the Röti summit.

Best period: April-November

Grade: strenuous, with an ascent of 900m/2950ft (of which the stretch shortly before Nesselboden is steep) and descent of 760m/2500ft (highest point 1321m, lowest 432m). If you include the Röti detour, add an additional 170m of ascent. But there are multiple ways to slice, dice and spice this walk, according to your tempo and gusto.

Equipment: hiking boots

Refreshments/accommodation: Restaurant Einsiedelei (closed Mon/Tue) at the end of the Verena Gorge; Kurhaus Weissenstein on Mount Weissenstein (hotel/restaurant, visible from Solothurn, scenic terrace, garden with some 150 local plants, long orientation table with names of Alpine mountains, (032 628 61 61, www.hotel-weissenstein.ch); Bergrestaurant Sennhaus (meals/snacks, closed Mon) just below the Kurhaus; Restaurant Hinter Weissenstein (about 2km west of the Kurhaus, closed Mon/Tue); Weberhüsli (restaurant), near the valley station of the chairlift

Transport: 🚌 direct trains run to Solothurn from Zurich, Biel and Olten; change trains at Solothurn for Oberdorf (departures 1-2 times/hour; journey time 12min). Shorter walks (see below) make use of the two-stage 🚡 chairlift from Oberdorf up to Kurhaus Weissenstein; you can also get on/off at the intermediate station Nesselboden (runs daily throughout the year, but out of action for four weeks in Mar/

Apr and Nov/Dec for maintenance, (032 626 46 00 or (032 622 18 27, www. seilbahnweissenstein.ch.

🚗: take exit 41 (Solothurn) off the A1 motorway to join the A5 motorway. Leave the A5 at exit 33 (Solothurn-Ost); three large underground car parks (Baseltor, Bieltor and Berntor) just outside Solothurn's old town.

Nearest accommodation: hotels, youth hostel in Solothurn; Kurhaus Weissenstein on Mount Weissenstein

Shorter walks

1 Solothurn to Weissenstein, descent with chairlift
(3h10min, access and grade as main walk, with an ascent of 900m). Follow the main walk up Mount Weissenstein, but take the 🚠 chairlift next to the Kurhaus Weissenstein to descend to Oberdorf, then 🚌 from Oberdorf to Solothurn.

2 Oberdorf to Weissenstein
(3h35min, ascent 670m, access by 🚌 to Oberdorf). Walk up the road towards Weissenstein for 250m, then turn right opposite the car park for the Weberhüsli restaurant *(no signposting)*. Follow this gravel forest road for 600m/10min, then take the path which climbs to your left *(no signposting)*. Once you reach the surfaced road, follow it to the right for 100m, to a hairpin bend. Go straight ahead here. The track, then path gently gains height and meets the signposted STIGENLOS junction (805m, 35min), from where you start the steep zigzag ascent, picking up the main walk at the 1h50min-point.

3 Oberdorf to Weissenstein, with chairlift (times below, access as for Shorter walk 2 above). At Oberdorf, you could take the 🚠 chairlift to the top of Weissenstein and walk back to Oberdorf station via Hinter Weissenstein (1h40min). Alternatively, walk up to Weissenstein as in Shorter walk 2 (1h55min), then take the chairlift back to Oberdorf station.

4 Verena Gorge (30min, ascent 50m). Just walk through the gorge — and use the bus to avoid the streets in Solothurn. From the front of Solothurn's railway station (but on the opposite side of the street) take 🚌 4 (terminus Rüttenen). Get off at St Niklaus, then walk west along the street, with an old peoples' home (Alterszentrum) on your left. After 100m turn right to enter the gorge

In the Verena Gorge

(sign: WENGISTEIN, 455m). Pick up the main walk at the 30min-point and leave it 10 minutes after Restaurant Einsiedelei, to get on the bus (www.bsu.ch) at Brüggmoos stop and return to Solothurn.

5 Stroll through Solothurn (time immaterial). Don't miss wandering around the old town — Switzerland's most baroque city. In the summer, tourist boats ply the Aare between Biel/Bienne and Solothurn.

W hat the Matterhorn is to Zermatt, the Eiger to Grindelwald or Salève to Geneva, Weissenstein is to Solothurn, the capital of the canton to which this town gives its name. Weissenstein's vertical white cliffs can be seen from far away, and from the summit there is a superb panorama.

From the railway station (432m) in **Solothurn**, take RÖTISTRASSE and cross the **Aare**, the river that flows through Solothurn, via the **Rötibrücke** (the bridge you see when facing away from the station). On your left is the old

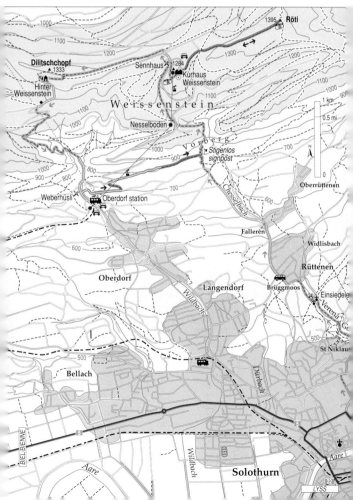

town of Solothurn with the mighty **Cathedral of St Ursen**. Follow the excellent signposting towards *WEISSENSTEIN*, to wander through the residential area of Solothurn.

Before long, you come to the **Verena Gorge** (Verenaschlucht; 2km from the railway station, **30min**, signpost *WENGISTEIN*, 455m). The marked trail meanders through woodland beside the Verena stream with its little waterfalls — a soothing stroll. Close to the end of the gorge you pass a **hermitage** ('Einsiedelei' in German; there are two chapels). Keep straight on towards a restaurant, *EINSIE-DELEI* (435m, **45min**). Turn left and, 25m further on, turn right.

The waymarked trail follows the roadside pavement to circle to the west of **Rüttenen**. Some 200m along the through road you come to the Brüggmoos *BUS STOP*, on your left. *(Shorter walk 4 returns to Solothurn from here.)* Past Rüttemen, you reach the hamlet of **Falleren** and a farm, the **Fallernhof**. From the signpost *FALLEREN* (555m, **1h05min**) take the middle of three gravel forestry roads, rising into the forest. The road peters out into a footpath that climbs very steeply in zigzags up through the gorge forged by the **Chesselbach** stream. There are some benches along the way, where you can take a break! During the climb you pass a signpost, *STIGENLOS* (805m, **1h50min**). *(Shorter walk 2 joins the main walk at this signpost.)* Once the strenuous ascent is behind you, continue straight on at a signposted junction (992m, **2h25min**) and climb

more gently through the small valley between the mountains of Vorberg and Weissenstein. You leave the forest for a short while at the intermediate station of the *CHAIRLIFT* from Oberdorf to Weissenstein (**Nesselboden**; 1057m, **2h35min**). Then the trail dives back into the forest, to emerge at the *BERGRESTAURANT SENN-HAUS* (1255m, 3h05min). Opposite is a *FIRST SUMMIT* on **Mount Weissenstein**, with the *KURHAUS WEISSENSTEIN* (hotel and restaurant; 1284m; **3h10min**), from where you enjoy a fantastic view of the Alps. Those with plenty of stamina can take a 1h return detour east from here to **Röti** (1395m), the *HIGHEST POINT* on the mountain.

From Kurhaus Weissenstein, retrace your steps to the road. There are various parallel paths which lead to the next landfall, the farm and restaurant Hinter Weissenstein. Walk along the road for about 150m, to the point where the road bends 90° to the right. Climb the steps here, to a path in the forest. This rises to 1321m and then descends to **Hinter Weissenstein** (1226m, **3h45min**).

From the farm, walk 100m along the gravel road, then turn right. The road bends right, to a **BARN**. A few metres past the barn, at a signpost, *HINTERWEISSENSTEIN* (1182m, **3h55min**) bear left. The steepish path brings you to the mountain pass road (768m, **4h40min**), where you turn right, past the Weberhüsli restaurant, to the valley station of the chairlift, next to the **Oberdorf** railway station (655m, **4h50min**). Return to Solothurn by train.

Walk 13 (Fribourg Alps): GRUYERES AND GRUYERE

Distance/time: 13km/8mi; 4h15min

Best period: any time of year, even if there is some snow

Grade: easy-moderate, with an ascent of 570m/1870ft; highest point 1232m, lowest 737m

Equipment: hiking boots

Refreshments and accommodation: Moléson-Village, Gruyères

Transport: 🚃 to Gruyères-Pringy railway station (746m), on the Bulle–Gruyères-Pringy line, hourly departures. 🚌 to Pringy-Gruyères (7km from Bulle). Gruyères is very touristic; there are three parking areas as one goes up the hill on the approach, as well as at the Gruyères-Pringy railway station. Moléson-Village, a small winter sports resort, has parking for 500 cars.

Shorter walks: I suggest four possibilities for halving the distance walked by using the bus to start or return: 🚐 from Gruyères-Pringy railway station to Moléson-Village (also called Moléson-sur-Gruyères), 7-9 departures a day, journey time 15min (there are also some buses from Bulle). For either half allow about 2h15min to ascend and a bit less than 2h to descend.

(1) Follow the main walk up from Pringy to Moléson-Village, descend by bus.

(2) Ascend from Pringy to Moléson-Village on the main walk *return* path: starting from the railway station, cross the car park, turn left, and a few metres further on, turn right on the main road up to Moléson-Village. Keep to this for 100m, then turn left just in front of the little church *(signposting is not obvious here)*. Follow the railway tracks to the few houses of Le Pas, then turn right. The rest is straightforward. Return by bus.

(3) and **(4)** Take a bus from

Pringy to Moléson-Village, then either follow the main walk from about the 2h20min- point to the end, or use the map to walk down via the *ascent* route.

Switzerland and cheese — here we go. But don't get confused: *La* Gruyère is a district in the Alpine foothills with verdant pastures; *Le* Gruyère is the world-famous hard yellow cheese made from cow's milk; Gruyères (with an 's') is the village — a market place in medieval times and a bustling tourism centre today. The circuit described below is the 'Sentier des Fromageries', the 'Cheese-dairy Walk', from Pringy-Gruyères (746m) to Moléson-Village (1107m) and back. Along the way, some 20 information panels let you in on the secrets of cheese-making. Be sure to visit the Maison du Gruyère opposite the railway station in Gruyères-Pringy (a show cheese-dairy with exhibitions, open daily from 9.00-18.00) and the similar Fromagerie d'Alpage (1132m) in Moléson-Village (daily mid-May to mid-October).

Two approaches to Moléson-Village are signposted at the Pringy-Gruyères railway station: this walk takes the anti-clockwise ascent ('Moléson-Village par la Pro-vêta'), so that Mount Moléson is in view during the climb; you will *return* through forest via the clockwise ascent trail ('Moléson-Village par la Forêt de Chésalles' and 'Parcours par les Reybes').

From the **Gruyères-Pringy** railway station (746m), cross the car park (walking away from the railway line). Turn right and walk on the pavement for about 100m, then cross the street at the restaurant Pinte des Vernes. Walk up surfaced ROUTE DES VERNES for 600m, then cross the **Albeuve** (**10min**). Walk through forest and past a few houses on the outskirts of Pringy. The ascent then continues through a picture-book landscape, with the mighty Moléson (Walk 14) in view most of the time. Ignore the junction for Le Pâquier and continue straight

Gruyères with its castle, shortly before reaching Moléson-Village

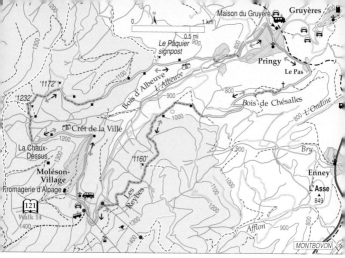

This walk is a real joy after a fresh fall of snow. On the ascent, Mount Moléson is in view for most of the way.

On the descent to Moléson-Village, you have a beautiful view over Gruyères with its castle. North of the village, the path kinks to the right (1129m, **2h05min**). Most of the houses of **Moléson-Village** are on your right as you approach the large parking area past the tiny (4m x 4m!) PYRAMIDAL CHURCH (1107m, **2h20min**).

After visiting (or not) the Fromagerie d'Alpage up to your right, continue along the road which descends to Pringy. But a few metres after the first hairpin bend, branch off right on a rising path (**2h30min**). This trail sidles up to a junction (SIGNPOST; 1160m, **2h50min**), where you keep straight ahead. After a short while the path descends through forest. When it comes into pastures again, take the right-hand fork after passing a POND at 967m (**3h15min**). Now the walk heads mostly through forest to a handful of houses close to the railway line (**Le Pas**, 737m, **4h**). Follow the road back to the **Gruyères-Pringy** railway station (**4h15min**).

ahead (984m, **50min**). When you come to another junction (SIGNPOST; 1172m, **1h30min**) turn left, and turn left again at the next junction (SIGNPOST; 1232m, **1h40min**). This latter junction is the highest point of the walk.

Walk 14 (Fribourg Alps): MOLESON

Distance/time: 17km/10.5mi; 6h15min (but can be cut to anywhere between 45min-2h30min; see Shorter walk 1 below)

Best period: June-October

Grade: strenuous: the first part from Moléson-Village to Plan-Francey is steepish; the climb from Petit Plané to the Moléson summit is strenuous. Ascent 1050m/3445ft; highest point 2002m, lowest 1107m

Equipment: hiking boots

Refreshments/accommodation: Hotel-Restaurant de Plan-Francey at the station between the funicular and cable car, a mountain lodge (rooms and dormitories), ☎ 026 921 10 42, www.plan-francey.ch; Restaurant de l'Observatoire on the Moléson summit (with 50 dormitory places and an observatory for thrilling views of the night sky), ☎ 026 921 29 96); Chalet-Restaurant at Gros Plané.

Transport: starting point is Moléson-Village (also called Moléson-sur-Gruyères); see Walk 13 on page 188.

Shorter walks

1 Moléson with funicular and/or cable car — up and/or down (times and ascents below). A funicular runs from Moléson-Village to Plan-Francey, and a cable car from Plan-Francey to the top of the Moléson. In summer they run daily from 09.00-18.00; on Fri and Sat from Jul-Sep they run later — until 23.00. They afford many ways to shorten the walk. The following times and ascents should help you plan your walk: (a) Moléson-Village to Plan-Francey: 1h25min, ascent 410m; (b) Plan-Francey to Moléson summit: 1h35min, ascent 540m, descent 50m; (c) Moléson summit to Plan-Francey: 2h30min, ascent 130m, descent 610m; (d) Plan-Francey to Moléson-Village: 45min, descent 410m.

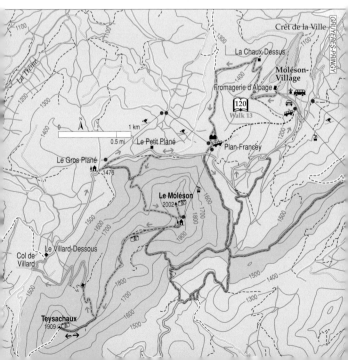

2 Moléson ridge (1h40min, quite easy, with an ascent of 240m. Take the funicular and cable car to the Moléson summit. Walk on the gently undulating path along the ridge — perhaps to the foot of Mount Teysachaux (1783m) and back.

Alternative walk: Teysachaux (2h40min, ascent 270m, only suitable for *experienced mountain hikers*). Follow Shorter walk 2 to the foot of Teysachaux. From there a very steep trail *(not waymarked)* rises 130m in height to the top — at 1909m.

Moléson, although not the highest, is the most famous mountain in the Fribourg Alps. It is a mighty, somewhat detached chunk of rock, as you can see in the photograph on page 120. There's even a famous folk song, 'To Moléson! To Moléson!' in its honour — saying more or less 'If you're fit enough to climb this mountain, don't miss it'. The song goes on to assure you that from the top of Moléson you will see the vast world. How true.

From the very large parking area at **Moléson-Village**, walk on towards the centre, a collection of newly-built chalets. A gravel path a few metres from the tiny (4m x 4m!) PYRAMIDAL CHAPEL (1107m) leads to an Alpine cheese-dairy (**Fromagerie d'Alpage**). Keep straight ahead across pastures — a SIGNPOST is clearly visible about 150m from the dairy. Take the quite-steeply rising earthen trail; it then kinks

north and takes you to the chalet **La Chaux-Dessus** (1369m, **45min**).

From here follow the gravel path to **Plan-Francey** (1520m, **1h25min**), the intermediate station between the funicular and cable car. Descend 150m to an ORIENTATION MAP (1497m), then head right (west) along the wide dirt road (*don't* follow the trail signposted 'Via Ferrata'). Ignore the trail which goes off to the left five minutes later.

When you are about 150m short of the cabin **Petit Plané** (1478m), take the trail ascending to the left (20m past a signpost; **1h35min**). The climb to the Moléson summit is straightforward but demanding. From the top station of the cable car (with restaurant) it is just five minutes to the SUMMIT OF **Moléson** (2002m, **3h**).

Return from here to the ridge trail below the restaurant — with gorgeous views on all sides, including Lake Geneva. The trail rises and falls gently, but finally descends to about 1788m at the foot of Mount Teysachaux (**3h45min**; see Alternative walk).

Turn right here, to descend to a CHALET (1689m). Then take the surfaced road, descending in wide switchbacks to the signposted **Col de Villard** (1459m, **4h25min**). Turn right and, still on surfaced road, come to the Chalet **Le Villard-Dessous** (1429m). Proceed straight on and tackle the gentle climb on a gravel and dirt road to the Chalet **Gros Plané** (1476m, **5h**). Don't continue on the road here, but bear right on the ascending path (signposted a few metres from the chalet). Gravel at the outset, the path then runs across pastures and quickly widens out into a dirt road. You pass the chalet **Petit Plané** (1478m) and emerge back at **Plan-Francey** (**5h30min**). Continue straight ahead on the gravel road, past the ORIENTATION MAP and below the cable car. Follow the SIGNS to **Moléson-Village** (**6h15min**).

Alternative walk: hikers on the last stretch of the ascent to the Teysachaux summit. The main walk follows the Moléson ridge (the sloping ridge at the left in the photograph).

Walk 15 (Vaud Alps): LAC RETAUD AND LA PALETTE

See also photograph on pages 34-35

Distance/time: 11km/6.8mi; 4h15min

Best period: June to October

Grade: easy-moderate. Ascent 630m/2065ft; highest point 2171m, lowest 1546m

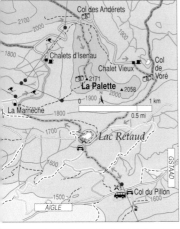

Equipment: hiking boots

Refreshments/accommodation: restaurants at the Col du Pillon and Lake Retaud. Refreshments also available at the Chalets d'Isenau and the Chalet Vieux. Accommodation in the village of Les Diablerets. (Les Diablerets is also the name of a mountain and its ski resort. Summer skiing is possible on the Diablerets glacier, the Glacier de Tsanfleuron, also known as 'Glacier 3000' because its elevation is 3000m; there is a cable car to the top.)

Transport: 🚆 to Aigle (Lausanne–Aigle line, journey time 30min), then take the little mountain 🚆 from Aigle to Les Diablerets *village* (journey time 48min), then 🚐 to the Col du Pillon (runs hourly, journey time 15min). Or 🚌 from Berne, Spiez or

Zweisimmen to Gstaad, then 🚌 to the Col du Pillon (5-6 departures/ day, journey time 34min). 🚗: exit 17 (Aigle) off the A9 motorway between Lausanne and Martigny, then drive from Aigle to the large parking area on the Col du Pillon (24km, 30min). Or drive up from Gstaad (18km, 30min).

Shorter walks

1 Loop omitting La Palette (3h15min, fairly easy, with an ascent of 500m). Follow the main walk, but omit the detour from the Col des Andérets to La Palette.

2 Start from Lac Retaud (3h30min, fairly easy ascent of 500m if you include La Palette; 2h30min — even easier ascent of 350m if you omit it). Access by 🚗: 100m from the Col du Pillon (towards the village of Les Diablerets) take the narrow road forking right; this leads up to the lake after 1.8km (parking area). Follow the main walk from the 25min-point to the 3h55min-point.

L ovely and fairly easy — a walk for everyone. You cross flower-filled pastures dotted with chalets where you can stop for a drink and some cheese, and you pass a splendidly sited lake, ideal for a swim. The shortest walk above only takes 2h30min, but this great mountain scenery is compelling, so allow a full day!

From the **Col du Pillon** (1546m), walk north, passing the bottom station of the CABLE CAR and follow sign-

posting up a mountain path through a bit of forest and pastures to **Lac Retaud** (1685m, **25min**, swimming in the summer).

Go between the restaurant and the lake and continue the ascent, to reach a farm, **La Marnèche** (1800m, **1h**). From there take the surfaced road past the **Chalets d'Isenau** (1855m, **1h15min**, refreshments) before reaching (now on a gravel road) the **Col des Andérets** (2034m, **1h50min**). The Arnensee (lake) is visible in the northeast from this pass.

From here the main walk makes a diversion to La Palette: after the signpost 'COL DES ANDERETS', continue on the gravel road for a few metres, then take the trail off

The route from the Col de Voré to Lac Retaud offers fine views to the massif of Les Diablerets and its foothills.

right, crossing meadows to the top of **La Palette** (2171m, **2h25min**), from where there is a gorgeous view to the massif of Les Diablerets and Lac Retaud just below.

Back at the **Col des Andérets** (**2h50min**), continue to the **Chalet Vieux** (1950m, **3h20min**; cheese and drinks) and the **Col de Voré** (1918m, **3h25min**). The lovely tarn here (un-named, but it deserves one!) marks the border between the Vaud and Berne cantons. At the Col de Voré, turn right and continue the descent to **Lac Retaud** (**3h55min**) and from there back to the **Col du Pillon**

Lac Retaud from the summit of La Palette

Walk 16 (Bernese Oberland): FIRST, FAULHORN AND SCHYNIGE PLATTE

Distance/time: 16km/10mi; 6h10min, but see Shorter walks below

Best period: June to October

Grade: strenuous, but technically easy. Ascent 700m/2300ft, descent 900m/2950ft; highest point 2681m, lowest 1933m. Signposts and hordes of tourists ensure you won't get lost! Make sure the weather is good.

Equipment: hiking boots

Refreshments/accommodation: Berghaus First at First mountain station (restaurant, rooms, dormitories, (033 853 12 84, www.berghausfirst.ch); Berghotel Faulhorn (open end Jun to mid-Oct, 6 rooms with 2-3 beds, 2 dormitories with 30 places each, often full at weekends, (033 853 27 13, www.berghotel-faulhorn.ch); Alpine hut Männdlenen/ Weberhütte (open end Jun to mid-Oct, 25 dormitory places, (033 853 44 64, www. berghaus-maenndlenen.ch); Hotel Schynige Platte (open end May to end Oct, singles/ doubles, (033 828 73 73, www.schynigeplatte.ch)

Transport: 🚠 up to First (2166m), reached from Grindelwald via a 6-seat gondola (mid-May to Oct, 25min ride); return by 🚞 cog railway to Wilderswil from Schynige Platte (Jun-Oct, up to 15 times/day, journey time 52min, last train at about 18.00), then 🚌 back to Grindelwald (runs almost every half hour, journey time 30min). A circular ticket can be bought which covers all three forms of transport.

Shorter walks

1 First — Bachsee — First (1h45min, ascent 170m, easy). Follow the main walk to the 50min-point, then retrace your steps. A beautiful walk, suitable for everyone.

2 First — Faulhorn — First. (4h05min, ascent of 580m, moderate to strenuous, technically easy). Follow the main walk to Faulhorn (2h20min), then walk back to First.

3 Two-day walk (time and ascent as main walk). Break the walk with an overnight stay at Faulhorn or Männdlenen.

This walk is a classic in the Bernese Oberland, and rightfully so. Legion are the hikers who cross from First to Schynige Platte (or vice versa) — among some of the most splendid scenery in the Alps. This high traverse runs entirely above the tree line, so pay attention to the weather forecast when you choose your day!

From **First** cable car station (2166m), take the gravel road signposted to BACHSEE (also called Bachalpsee), passing the Gummi-Hütte (more of a shed; **30min**). The view across the lake (**Bachsee**; 2265m, **50min**) to Schreckhorn (4078m) and Finsteraarhorn (4274m) is the epitome of an Alpine panorama. *(Shorter*

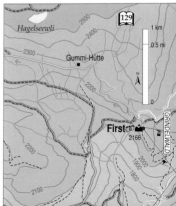

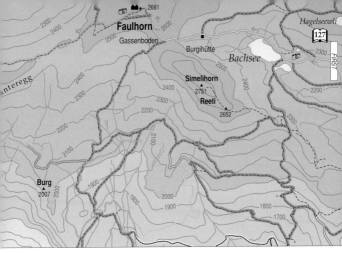

Left: wrapped in veils of mist — the mysterious Eiger north face; below left: the Schynige Platte cog railway

walk 1 turns back to First from here.)

You pass the **Burgihütte** (another shed, 2438m, **1h40min**) and turn right at a junction called **Gassenboden** (2553m, **1h55min**), to arrive at the SUMMIT OF **Faulhorn** (2681m, **2h20min**). Here, at the top, is the Berghotel Faulhorn, built in 1830 — making it the oldest mountain hotel in the Alps. It's great to stay overnight here and watch the spectacle of a sunset and sunrise, but telephone reservations are a must!

The views are spectacular as you continue below Faulhorn: the white trio of Eiger, Mönch and Jungfrau rise to the south, and Lake Brienz lies 2000m below you to the north. After the trail swings to the right, you arrive at the **Männdlenen Hut** (2344m, **3h20min**) — another good place to stay during a two-day walk.

Some 15 minutes past the hut, the path makes a left turn into a long valley, the **Sägistal**, completely enclosed by ridges.

The trail eventually rounds **Mount Loucherhorn** (signpost: LAUCHEREN, 2020m, **4h50min**). A couple of minutes later you arrive at a junction where you have the choice of taking a direct path to Schynige Platte (saving 40 minutes) or the longer, well-named 'Panorama Trail' which offers dizzying views down over Lake Brienz and Lake Thun.

The main walk bears right for the **Panoramaweg**. The path is safe, but at times there are sheer drops just a few metres away. At a junction below **Mount Oberberghorn** (2069m, **5h20min**) bear right again, to stay on the Panoramaweg. (By the way, Oberberghorn can be climbed; there are ladders.)

You pass the place called **Daube** (SIGNPOST: 2076m, **5h45min**) and finally arrive at **Schynige Platte** (1980m, **6h10min**). If you feel you haven't already had enough exercise, instead of taking the cog railway from Schynige Platte, you can walk down (mostly through forest) to the Breitlauenen railway station (1542m) in just an hour.

129

Walk 17 (Bernese Oberland): SCHWARZHORN

See also photograph page 10
Distance/time: 13km/8mi; 6h15min
Best period: June to October
Grade: Strenuous and *technically challenging:* you must be sure-footed and have a head for heights. Ascent 1030m/3380ft; highest point 2928m, lowest 1962m. The walk is entirely above the tree line, so there is *no shade.* Make sure the weather is good because there are *no shelters on the way.*
Equipment: hiking boots
Refreshments/accommodation: Hotel Grosse Scheidegg (closed in winter, (033 853 67 16, www.grosse-scheidegg.ch) at the start, *nothing en route*
Transport: post 🚌 from Grindelwald to Grosse Scheidegg (1962m). 🚗: cars

are only allowed as far as the Hotel Wetterhorn (1230m, open all year, large car park, (033 853 12 18, www.grosse-scheidegg.ch)
Alternative walks: A classic walk in the area leads from Meiringen in the Hasli Valley up to Grosse Scheidegg and then down to Grindelwald. You could follow this route *downhill* from Grosse Scheidegg — heading west via Stepfihubel to Grindelwald (2h30min, descent 930m). Another walk from Grosse Scheidegg to Grindelwald cuts across the winding road. Both walks are downhill all the way. Although they are well signposted and waymarked, the appropriate map would be helpful (see page 67).

The highest mountain north of Grindelwald, Schwarzhorn offers splendid views onto the icy, rocky masses south of Grindelwald — especially to Wetterhorn (3692m) directly opposite Schwarzhorn.

The ride with the post bus from Grindelwald (or the Hotel Wetterhorn) sets the tone for a great day out, as the bus honks its melodious horn (from the *William Tell* overture; see page 9) while zigzagging up the narrow road from the Hotel Wetterhorn to Grosse Scheidegg.

From **Grosse Scheidegg** (1962m), take the gravel road northwest towards SCHWARZHORN. At the **Gratschärem** junction (SIGNPOST; 2006m, **25min**), one path turns right, two others branch left. Take

View south from near Chrinnenboden; Schilt is the 'dinosaur' ridge on the right.

On the way from Grosse Scheidegg to Grindelwald (Alternative walk)

the middle path of the three. This rises to 2030m and then drops to 1970m at the next signposted junction (**50min**), above the dozen or so huts of the settlement **Grindelwald-Oberläger**.

Now the ascent gets more serious. Bear right and, accompanied by the sound of cowbells, follow the trail across mountain pastures to the **Chrinnenboden** junction (SIGNPOST; 2241m,

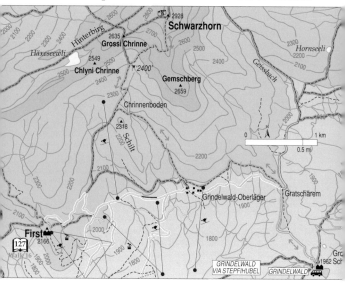

1h45min). Turn right here, continuing the ascent through ever-thinner vegetation.
At the next junction (SIGNPOST; 2400m, **2h15min**), turn right (where the *via ferrata* route forks left). The trail snakes up steadily over bare rock, and you eventually reach the SCHWARZHORN RIDGE

(**3h15min**). As you get closer to the top, there are a few exposed passages (at one point a handrail helps). Enjoy the view from the SUMMIT OF **Schwarzhorn** (**3h50min**) — you deserve it!
Then walk back down the same way to **Grosse Scheidegg** (**6h15min**).

Two hikers on the Schwarzhorn ridge; note the exposed trail.

Distance/time: almost 20km/ 12.5mi; 6h55min for the entire trail, but can be broken down to stretches lasting from 1h20min to 4h20min (see Shorter walks below).

Best period: June to October

Grade: easy to strenuous. The section from Männlichen to Kleine Scheidegg is a doddle and one of the busiest walks in the Alps — with absolutely stunning scenery. For the stretch from Kleine Scheidegg back to Grindelwald, you must be sure-footed, although it is technically easy. The ascent over the entire trail is 390m/ 1280ft, the descent 1670m/ 5475ft; highest point 2343m, lowest 937m. The 'Eigertrail' itself runs from Eigergletscher station (2320m) to Alpiglen (1616m) and is mostly walked in the direction described here, that is, downhill.

Equipment: hiking boots

Refreshments/accommodation: Restaurant/Hotel Männlichen (2229m, (033 853 10 68). Kleine Scheidegg comprises a railway station (as bustling as a busy city station!) and a few hotels: Bellevue des Alpes ((033 855 12 12, www. scheidegg-hotels.ch); Bahnhof Kleine Scheidegg (rooms and dormitories, (033 828 78 28); Grindelwaldblick (5min from Kleine Scheidegg, dormitories, (033 855 13 74, www.grindel waldblick.ch). In Alpiglen there is the mountain inn Berghaus Alpiglen (rooms and dormitories, (033 853 11 30, www.alpiglen.ch).

Transport: 🚞 , 🚌 or 🚗 to the Männlichen lift station at Grund, part of Grindelwald (in the valley). The lift station is 400m northwest of the valley station of the cog railway that rises to Kleine Scheidegg (both stations are next to the river). There's a very large car park at Männlichen valley station. Then 🚡 gondola lift up to Männlichen station (30min).

Shorter walks

1 Männlichen to Kleine Scheidegg (1h20min, descent 170m). This downhill walk is short, simple, spectacular, stunning. Access as main walk; follow the main walk to the 1h20min-point, then take the Jungfrau 🚞 cog railway back to Grindelwald). You can also do this walk from Wengen (take the cable car from there to Männlichen and the cog railway back to Wengen).

2 Kleine Scheidegg (or Eigergletscher station) to Alpiglen (3h, ascent 340m, descent 790m from Kleine Scheidegg — 1h less from Eigergletscher station). From Grindelwald or Wengen, take the Jungfrau 🚞 cog railway to Kleine Scheidegg, then pick up the main walk at the 1h20min-point (or the 2h20min-point, if starting from Eigergletscher). At the Alpiglen junction (4h-point), descend left for 20min to Alpiglen (1616m) and return to Grindelwald or Wengen via cog railway.

3 Männlichen to Kleine Scheidegg, then Eigertrail to Alpiglen (4h20min, ascent 340m, descent 960m). This is Shorter walks 1 and 2 in succession.

4 Kleine Scheidegg to Grindelwald (5h25min, ascent 390m, descent 1500m). Take the Jungfrau 🚞 cog railway from Grindelwald to Kleine Scheidegg, then pick up the main walk at the 1h20min-point and follow it all he way back to Grund in Grindelwald.

The Eiger north face of the 'triumvirate' Eiger (3970m), Mönch (4107m) and Jungfrau (4158m) is one of the world's most famous walls. No rock face has more recorded history of tragedy and triumph. The walk described below is among the finest in the Alps. Undertaking the entire hike is strenuous, although not particularly difficult. But it can easily be broken into various stretches that allow the epicure to savour one of the greatest Alpine experiences at a leisurely pace.

Before starting the walk, make a worthwhile 30-minute return detour north from **Männlichen** STATION (2229m) to the top of **Männlichen** (2343m, fine views, ORIENTATION TABLE). Then return and take the wide path from the station (2229m, **0min**) via **Rotstöckli** (2110m, **1h10min**) to **Kleine Scheidegg** (2061m, **1h20min**). From here the walk more or less follows the Jungfrau cog railway line (you could take it to Eigergletscher, the next station!). At a junction (SIGN-POST; 2203m, **1h50min**) you *could* just fork left beside the railway line, but the main walk goes straight on here, then bends left and crosses moraine to approach **Eigergletscher** STATION (2320m, **2h20min**) from the south.

This is where the Eigertrail proper starts — just where the train vanishes into the mountain, never to surface again until it reaches the Jungfraujoch at 3454m. Go up the surfaced path to the buildings. A gradually descending foot-

View from Männlichen into the Lauterbrunnen Valley

path (with one intervening short ascent of 50m) takes you across scree and through sparse vegetation alongside the lower on your left there are sweeping views. There are no forks to worry you for well over 90 minutes — until you arrive at

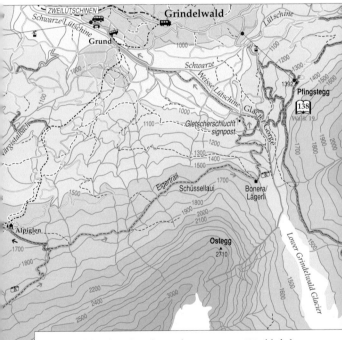

slopes of the sheer 'mother of all walls' — the north face of the Eiger. You are almost in physical contact with the wall on the right; the JUNCTION FOR **Alpiglen** (1725m, **4h**; *on the official Swiss maps shown as 1758m.*) The main walk turns right here, to continue on a fascinating high-

level trail. *(But for Shorter walks 2 or 3, descend left.)*
You now traverse the northeast flank of the Eiger. Vegetation becomes abundant, and you eventually enter forest. Pass the **Schüssellaui** SIGNPOST (**5h**), brave a slightly exposed stretch of path (**5h10min**) and arrive at a log cabin (**Bonera/Lägerli**, 1508m, **5h30min**).
Descend a ladder (**5h50min**) and soon catch a glimpse of the lower Grindelwald glacier. At a junction (1137m, **6h10**) turn right for GLETSCHERSCHLUCHT (glacier gorge), then go left at the fork a couple of minutes later (same sign). From the **Gletscherschlucht** SIGNPOST (1014m, **6h20min**) head along the river towards GRINDELWALD/ GRUND, to get to the **Grund** RAILWAY STATION (943m, **6h50min**) or GONDOLA STATION (937m, **6h55min**).

View of Eiger (left) and Mönch, on the way to Kleine Scheidegg

Walk 19 (Bernese Oberland): PFINGSTEGG AND BÄREGG

Distance/time: 5km/3mi; 2h30min
Best period: June to October
Grade: easy, but you must have a certain head for heights. Ascent 380m/1245ft, highest point 1770m, lowest 1370m. *Note that* older maps — and some signs — still show this trail passing by a hut at Stieregg (1650m). But that old hut was in danger of falling into the abyss, so was deliberately burned down. The trail now ends at the newly built Bäregg hut (1770m), just a short way to the north.
Equipment: hiking boots
Refreshments/accommodation: Restaurant at the upper Pfingstegg cable car station; Bäregg hostel (4-6 bedrooms, 28 dormitory places, ☎ 033 853 43 14, www.baeregg.com)
Transport: 🚌, 🚗 or on foot to the parking area for the 🚠 Pfingsteggbahn (cable car). To get there, follow the main road through Grindelwald almost to its eastern end. After the church, bear right downhill for 200m. Take the cable car to the top station.
Alternative walk: Schreckhorn hut (about 7h, ascent 1300m). *This splendid Alpine route (see page 65) is only suitable for experienced mountain hikers.* Continue from the Bäregg hut towards the head of the valley. The point where the trail bends 90° left (Bänisegg,

Hut between Grindelwald and Pfingstegg

1808m) into the valley makes a fantastic picnic spot. As you proceed towards the Rots Gufer cliffs, the hike becomes more difficult as the trail makes its way up these cliffs, protected by cables and metal pegs (some ladders). Above the Rots Gufer traverse the going gets easier and you eventually reach the Schreckhorn hut (2529m, serviced end Jun-early Oct, 90 dormitory places, ☎ 033 855 10 25) about 3h above Bäregg. Return the same way.

This is a short and fairly easy walk that nevertheless brings you into close contact with mountains, gorges and glaciers. The path runs high above the gorge of the lower Grindelwald glacier and at times runs just a few metres from the edge of the sheer cliff. Those with no heads for heights may feel a bit uneasy occasionally, but the trail is wide and safe.

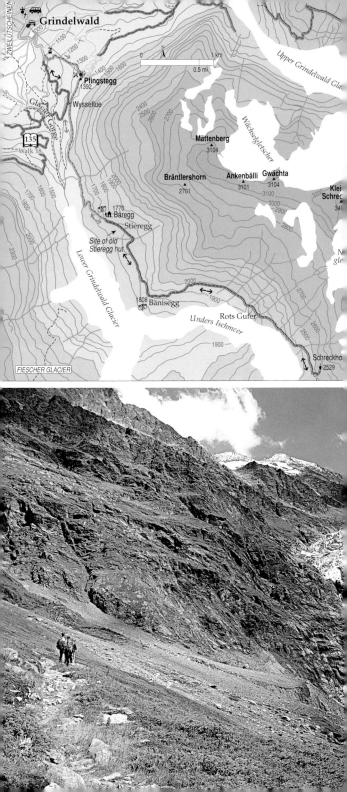

Grindelwald

Zweilütschinen

Pfingstegg
1392

Wyssefflue

Glacier Gorge

135
Walk 18

Bäregg
1770

Stieregg

Site of old
Stieregg hut

Lower Grindelwald Glacier

Bäniegg
1808

Unders Ischmeer

Rots Gufer

FIESCHER GLACIER

Mättenberg
3104

Bräntlershorn
2701

Ankenbälli
3101

Gwächta
3104

Wächselgletscher

Upper Grindelwald Gla

Klei
Schre

349

N
gle

Schreckho
2529

Walk 19 enters the valley from the left-hand side of the photograph. The snow-covered rock face to the right is the Eiger north face.

The main walk starts at the TOP STATION of the **Pfingstegg** cable car (1392m). (You could walk up here from Grindelwald: from the cable car parking area continue down the road and cross the river,

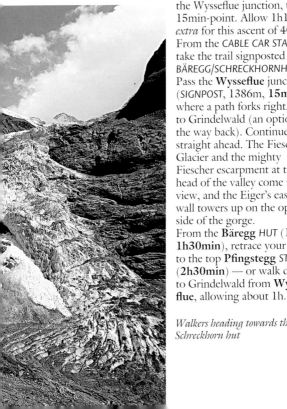

then take the signposted/ waymarked path which closely follows the cable car route and rises to Pfingstegg. About a third of the way up you could bear right at a junction, cutting out Pfingstegg and arriving at the Wysseflue junction, the 15min-point. Allow 1h15min *extra* for this ascent of 400m.) From the CABLE CAR STATION take the trail signposted BÄREGG/SCHRECKHORNHÜTTE. Pass the **Wysseflue** junction (SIGNPOST, 1386m, **15min**), where a path forks right, down to Grindelwald (an option on the way back). Continue straight ahead. The Fiescher Glacier and the mighty Fiescher escarpment at the head of the valley come into view, and the Eiger's eastern wall towers up on the opposite side of the gorge.
From the **Bäregg** HUT (1770m, **1h30min**), retrace your steps to the top **Pfingstegg** STATION (**2h30min**) — or walk down to Grindelwald from **Wysse-flue**, allowing about 1h.

Walkers heading towards the Schreckhorn hut

Walk 20 (Bernese Oberland): SCHILTHORN

Distance/time: 14km/8.7mi; 7h10min (or from 2h40min to 4h20min; see Shorter walks)
Best period: July to October
Grade: very strenuous but technically easy. Ascent 1350m/4430ft; highest point 2970m, lowest 1638m
Equipment: hiking boots
Refreshments/accommodation: Schilthorn hut (*not* at the summit, but at 2432m, open Jul-Sep, 25 places, (033 855 50 53); revolving restaurant (with cinema!) on the Schilthorn summit; refreshments at Schiltalp (1946m); plenty of accommodation in Mürren.

Transport: starting point is Mürren, a car-free village; see page 62, 'Lauterbrunnen • Mürren • Schilthorn' for access.

Shorter walks
1 Schilthorn: walk up, ride down (4h30min, ascent 1350m, grade as main walk). Follow the main walk to the 4h30min-point. The last ⛟ down leaves the Schilthorn summit at around 18.00.
2 Schilthorn: ride up, walk down (2h40min, descent 1350m, moderate). ⛟ to Schilthorn, then follow the main walk from the 4h30min-point.

Schilthorn rose to world fame as the film location for the James Bond film 'On Her Majesty's Secret Service' (a 10-minute clip from the film can be seen at the revolving restaurant on top of Schilthorn). But even without 007, Schilthorn is a mountain not to be missed: the 360° view from the summit is among the most fabulous in the Alps. The restaurant at the top goes through one revolution per hour, allowing you to

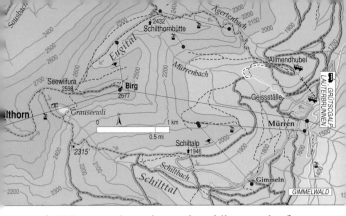

watch 200 mountain peaks pass by while you relax from the ascent. Only a few hardy hikers walk up here from Mürren, but naturally throngs come up by cable car.

From the *CABLE CAR STATION* in **Mürren** (1638m), follow signposting for *SCHILTHORN-HÜTTE/SCHILTHORN* and admire some of the village houses and gardens. Turn left at a junction (**5min**) and follow the waymarked route past *SIGN-POSTS* indicating the junctions **Geissställe** (1750m, **20min**) and **Allmendhubel** (1899m, **45min**) — this latter is just five minutes from a funicular station.

The path winds steadily upward through pastures to the **Schilthorn** *HUT* (2432m, **2h35min**) at the foot of the **Engital**. You then traverse this barren valley to reach the almost desert-like **Seewlifura** saddle (or Seelifuhre, 2598m, **3h20min**). Some 100m below you in height is Grauseewli (or Grauseeli), a lake which you'll pass on the way back. You tackle the final ascent to **Schilthorn** (2970m, **4h30min**) while you watch cable cars sailing to the top!

Retrace your steps towards the **Seewlifura** saddle, turn right and descend to the lake (**Grauseewli**, 2514m, **5h15min**). Then continue down towards *SCHILTALP*. At a junction (*SIGNPOST*: 2315m, **5h35min**), turn left to continue the descent through Alpine meadows to **Schiltalp** (1946m, **6h20min**), where you can admire the collection of bells on the front of the house. Following signposting, return via **Gimmeln** to **Mürren** (**7h10min**).

Grauseewli, with Jungfrau in the background

Walk 21 (Valais): VINEYARD TRAIL FROM MARTIGNY TO LEUK

See also photographs on pages 45 and 49
Distance/time: 60km/37mi — almost 20 hours, which can be covered over 2-5 days. The highest point of the trail is 800m, the lowest 450m, so there are no dramatic ascents/descents. The times given in the table overleaf are the times between adjacent villages, and they are usually about the same no matter which direction you are heading.
Best period: any time of year, but particularly lovely, of course, during grape harvest in September/October (if you ask the grape farmers whether you may taste some grapes, they will surely say yes).
Grade: easy and with good signposting (the signs are marked with a bunch of grapes resembling the canton's flag).
Equipment: hiking boots or training shoes
Refreshments/accommodations: in the wine villages along the way. Larger towns are Martigny (pop 15,000), Sion, the capital of Valais (pop 27,000) and Sierre (pop 14,000)
Transport: 🚌 to Martigny (Geneva–Brig line). Take the 🚌 post bus heading towards Sion from the Martigny railway station and alight at 'Branson, Pont du Rhône' (the fourth stop after the railway station, immediately after the bus has crossed the Rhône — just a four-minute ride). *Note: do not* confuse this stop with the 'Portes du Rhône' stop (the second stop on the bus route). Return by 🚌 from Leuk to

Martigny (many trains on this line). 🚗: exit 21 (Martigny) off the A9 motorway; parking area near the railway station
Shorter walks: This walk can basically be started and stopped anywhere, and it can be broken down into as many sections as you like. If you want to do it in two days with an overnight stop in Sion (halfway between Martigny and Leuk), you need to be in shape. Three to four days is a more leisurely pace. Alternatively, you can start the walk just about anywhere — either by taking the post 🚌 from Martigny to Sion which stops in all the wine villages along the trail — or by taking the 🚈 which traverses the valley (from the corresponding railway stations you can easily walk to the vineyard slopes).
Further information: The walk is described in detail in a booklet (French/German only,

View from the tower at Saillon

142

124 pages) which you can buy at tourist offices or from www. cheminduvignoble.ch or www. weinweg.ch. The table overleaf

(which replaces our usual map) is taken from the book (© Association Chemin du Vignoble). See also Car tour 7.

This is a beautiful walk in one of the sunniest parts of Switzerland. Vineyards, dotted with wine villages, stretch all the way from Martigny to Leuk. The trail mostly runs through the wine-growing areas — sometimes right through the vineyards themselves.

From the '**Pont du Rhône, Branson**' BUS STOP on the Rhône, walk a few paces to the PLACE DES FOLLATERES; then head up the hillside and turn right, to arrive at the village of **Branson** (notice the lovely *trompe-l'œil* on the façade of one of the houses). The path traverses the communities which comprise **Fully**: **Vers- l'Eglise, Châtagnier, Saxé** and **Mazembroz**. In Fully you walk through a magnificent chestnut forest. **Saillon**, with its castle ruins, is arguably the most picturesque village on the whole walk. The tower can be

climbed, with a wonderful view over the valley (see Car tour 7, pages 44 and 48, for details of Saillon).
Cross the **Salentse** stream and continue to **Leytron** and **Chamoson**, where the vine- yards snuggle against the vertical rock face. Between **Ardon** and **Magnot** the trail follows the busy canton road. Back in the vineyards, the next wine village is **Vétroz**, then the small settlements **Sensine** and **Vuisse**. Go through the hamlet of **La Muraz** with **Lake Mont d'Orge** nearby and approach Sion.

Chemin de randonnée pédestre —

	Temps ↓ Zeit	Temps ↑ Zeit		Altitude (m) Höhe (M)
Martigny (Pont de Branson)				461
	1h00	50		
Branson				526
	40	40		
Vers l'Eglise (Fully)				535
	15	20		
Châtaignier				485
	15	15		
Saxé				468
	10	10		
Mazembroz				490
	5	5		
Vieux Chêne				485
	50	50		
La Sarvaz				470
	15	15		
Saillon				510
	20	20		
Les Moulins (Gorges de la Salentse)				490
	30	25		
Leytron (à 10 min du chemin du vignoble)				570
	50	50		
Chamoson				640
	1h05	1h15		
Ardon				503
	10	10		
Magnot				487
	30	30		
Vétroz				497
	1h00	50		
Sensine (Conthey)				634
	15	20		
Vuisse (Savièse)				575
	40	35		
La Muraz				650
	40	40		
Sion				560
	1h35	1h40		
St-Léonard				508
	2h00	1h50		
Ollon				660
	35	35		
Corin de la Crête				666
	25	25		
Loc				682
	35	30		
Les Anchettes				761
	15	10		
Venthône				808
	30	35		
Miège				702
	30	30		
Salgesch (20 min vom Weinweg entfernt)				686
	1h30	1h25		
Varen				760
	45	45		
Leuk-Stadt				731
	20	25		
Leuk				624
Total	18h30	18h10		

Martigny

Sion

Sierre

Leuk

© association Chemin du Vignoble - www.bernard...

derweg — Walking trail

+41 27 720 49 49

+41 27 746 20 80

*1:25000
Du Rhône aux Muverans*

+41 27 743 11 88

+41 27 306 42 93

+41 27 306 55 33

*1:25000
Derborence-Sanetsch*

+41 27 346 72 01

+41 27 395 27 37

1:25000 - Anzère

+41 27 327 77 27

+41 27 485 04 04

*1:25000
Crans-Montana - Sierre*

+41 27 455 85 35

*1:25000
Leukerbad*

+41 27 473 10 94

couverture : Régis Colombo - 2e édition mars 2007

Sion is the capital of the Valais and has a pretty old town nuzzling against two prominent hills, Tourbillon and Valère. Although waymarked, the trail circling the north side of the town takes some finding! As you descend through vineyards towards Sion, turn sharp right close to the road which leaves Sion, and take the underpass to cross the road. About 150m after the underpass (entering the residential area), turn left. Follow this street for 300m, past a church on your left, to the ROUTE DU RAWYL which runs north/south through Sion. Cross this busy road (about 50m below the roundabout) and take the path at right angles to the road. The path turns left after 50m and quickly rises above Sion. (If you first explore Sion's old town, take the Route du Rawyl north until you are 50m below the roundabout, then follow the path as above.) After Sion, the trail runs high above the Rhône alongside an enchanting WATER CHANNEL, the **Bisse de Clavoz** — a highlight of the walk. Descend to the village **Uvrier** to cross the Liène stream, then rise again through adjacent **St-Léonard**. Go through **St Clément, Ollon, Champ-zabé** and **Corin-de-la-Crête**. Sierre is bypassed via the villages **Loc, Les Anchettes, Venthône** and **Miège**. Between Miège and **Salgesch**, the **Raspille** stream marks the French-German language border (so from now on, you are no longer on a *sentier* but a *Weg*). Don't descend to Salgesch, but follow another ancient IRRIGATION CHANNEL. Then descend via **Varen** and **Leuk**, to cross the **Rhône** and walk to Leuk's RAILWAY STATION.

Walk 22 (Valais): GREAT ST-BERNARD PASS

See also photograph page 52
Distance/time: 12km/7.5mi;
5h10min
Best period: June/July to
September (the rest of the year
the pass is covered in snow up
to tens of metres deep)
Grade: strenuous, high-level
circuit via three passes, only to
be undertaken in fine weather
conditions. Ascent 1050m/
3445ft; highest point 2754m,
lowest 2346m
Equipment: hiking boots —
and best to take your *passport!*
**Refreshments/accommoda-
tion:** only at the Hospice du
Grand St-Bernard on the pass
(rooms, dormitory; ✆ 027 787
12 36; www.gsbernard.ch)
Transport: 🚌 from Martigny

to the Great St-Bernard Pass
(transfer in Bourg-St-Pierre),
or 🚆 to Orsières (transfer in
Sembrancher), then 🚌 to the
pass (Jun-Sep only, three
buses/day, journey time about
1h30min). 🚗: drive via
Martigny (exit 22 off the A9
motorway) through the Val
d'Entremont on the old road
right up to the pass (*don't* enter
the long tunnel which bypasses
the Great St-Bernard Pass and
which is open throughout the
year); parking area on the pass.
**Shorter walk: Lacs de
Fenêtre** (4h, grade as main
walk, but ascent of 770m).
Follow the main walk to the
2h-point, have a picnic, then
return the same way.

The **Great St-Bernard Pass** (2469m; Col du Grand
St-Bernard in French, Colle del Gran San Bernardo
in Italian) connects Switzerland and Italy and is the
most ancient pass through the Western Alps, travelled
by pilgrims, traders and entire armies — from Julius
Caesar to Napoleon, who crossed the pass into Italy in
1800 with 40,000 men. Napoleon's bill with the hospice was not settled until 1984, when French President
Mitterand made a token gesture (see plaque in Bourg-
St-Pierre). A hospice on the pass for travellers, founded
almost a thousand years ago in 1049, is still operational.

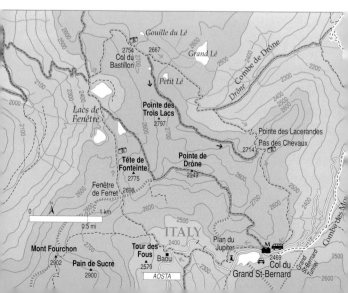

The stunningly beautiful Lacs de Fenêtre

There is a museum and a kennel for the famous St-Bernard dogs (open daily June-September). This is a fantastic hike above the tree line: lakes and mountain passes amidst majestic scenery in an historic setting.

From the hospice on the **Great St-Bernard Pass** (2469m), facing the lake, take the path running just above the right-hand side of the road behind the hotel. You cross the Swiss-Italian border and pass a statue (**Plan du Jupiter**; **10min**). Continue on the trail, crossing the road (**15min**). Descending, you cross the road once more (2358m, **30min**) shortly before a farm (**Baou**).

Now you begin the ascent to the first mountain pass: about 15min after the Baou farm, keep right at the fork. Once on the pass (**Fenêtre de Ferret**, 2698m, **1h30min**), you're back in Switzerland. From here you descend to three sparkling lakes, the **Lacs de Fenêtre**: go between the first two lakes and skirt the third lake clockwise. After the third lake (**2h**), keep right and start climbing to the second pass, the **Col du Bastillon** (2754m, **2h45min**). From here there is a magnificent view west to the roof of Europe — Mont Blanc at 4810m, while Grand Combin (4314m) rises to the east and the Lacs de Fenêtre shine below you.

Wander downhill. Ten minutes below the pass you have a choice: *either* continue down the waymarked trail for another 30 minutes and then fork right (**3h25min**) to tackle the steep 1h ascent to the Pas des Chevaux (**4h25min**), *or* take the narrow trail (*not waymarked*) forking off right, which reaches the Pas des Chevaux more directly.

From the **Pas des Chevaux** (2714m) return to the **Great St-Bernard Pass** (**5h10min**).

Walk 23 (Valais): LAKE MAUVOISIN

Distance/time: 21km/13mi; 7h (but see Shorter walks)
Best period: July to October
Grade: strenuous and long, but technically easy. Ascent 950m/3120ft; highest point 2628m, lowest 1841m
Equipment: hiking boots
Refreshments/accommoda- **tion:** Hotel Restaurant de Mauvoisin (close to the base of the dam, summer only, ℂ 027 778 11 30, www.mauvoisin. ch); Cabane de Chanrion (open Jul-Sep, also in winter but unstaffed, 100 dormitory places, ℂ 027 778 12 09)
Transport: 🚌 from Martigny

On the way back to the Mauvoisin Dam

to Le Châble, then 🚌 to
Fionnay (shortest journey time
Martigny–Fionnay 1h), then
🚌 from Fionnay to
Mauvoisin (3 times/day from
Jul–Sep; journey time 15min).
The time between the first bus
arriving at Mauvoisin and the
last bus departing from
Mauvoisin is just *under 7h*.
🚗: exit 22 (Grand St-Bernard)
off the A9 motorway at
Martigny. At Sembrancher,
pick up signs for Verbier. At
Le Châble you enter the Val de
Bagnes and, driving via
Fionnay, arrive at the car park
for the Hotel Restaurant de
Mauvoisin, not far from the
dam. You can also continue
through one more bend and
park a bit higher up.

Shorter walks
1 Mauvoisin Dam (time immaterial). Just going up to the
dam and rambling alongside
the lake and back for as long as
you like is good fun.
2 Lake Mauvoisin (4h, ascent
400m). Follow the main walk
to the southern end of the lake
and return the same way.
**3 Lake Mauvoisin and the
Tsofeiret Plateau** (6h15min,
ascent 820m). Follow the main
walk to the 2h10min-point,
but go *left* at this junction and
climb to the junction at 2524m
on the Tsofeiret Plateau. Pick
up the main walk again at the
4h55min-point).
4 Two-day walk: At the
halfway point, stay overnight
in the Cabane de Chanrion.

Lake Mauvoisin is a reservoir in the Val de Bagnes in
the canton of Valais. The reservoir was created by
the building of the Mauvoisin Dam in 1957 (see page
47). At a height of 250m, the dam, audaciously overhanging in the centre, is one of the world's highest arch
dams and the second highest dam in Switzerland
(Grande Dixence, visited on Walk 25, is the highest).
Several impressive waterfalls plunge into the lake.

From the HOTEL RESTAURANT
DE MAUVOISIN (1841m) head
south towards the reservoir
and go up the signposted trail,
passing a CHAPEL. Join the road
(**5min**) and follow it up
towards the lake, entering an
illuminated TUNNEL. At the
junction just inside the tunnel,
go left to visit the DAM WALL
for Shorter walk 1; for the
main walk, turn right and
continue through the tunnel
for 1km, crossing a thundering
stream.
Beyond the tunnel, the unsurfaced road follows the shore of
the lake — rising to a pasture
called **La Lia** (2115m, **1h**) and
then descending to the

SOUTHERN TIP OF THE LAKE
(1980m). At the junction
about five minutes past the lake
(SIGNPOST; **2h10min**) keep
right. *(But for Shorter walk 3, go
left here.)* Keep left at another
junction, to cross a bridge
(**Pont du Lancet**, 2049m,
2h25min). Two minutes later,
go right at the fork and begin a
zigzag ascent on a path which
cuts some bends off the road
(all the short-cuts are signposted). The walk levels off as
you approach the hut, the
Cabane de Chanrion
(2462m, **4h**), the southernmost point of our walk.
From here the trail heads north,
first crossing mountain pas-

tures, then scree, then a bridge over the stream draining water from the Brenay Glacier. Finally, there's a steepish ascent to the **Col de Tsofeiret** (2628m, **4h40min**), the highest point of the walk.

On the way down you soon pass the lovely **Lac de Tsofeiret** (2572m) on the high **Tsofeiret Plateau** and reach a junction (SIGNPOST; 2524m,

4h55min). *(Shorter walk 3 rejoins here.)* The path back to the dam now offers pretty views down over the lake. Near the Alpine meadow called **Giétro**, the trail meets an unsurfaced road (there are some waymarked short-cuts). After crossing the DAM WALL (**6h45min**), retrace your steps to the HOTEL RESTAURANT DE MAUVOISIN (**7h**).

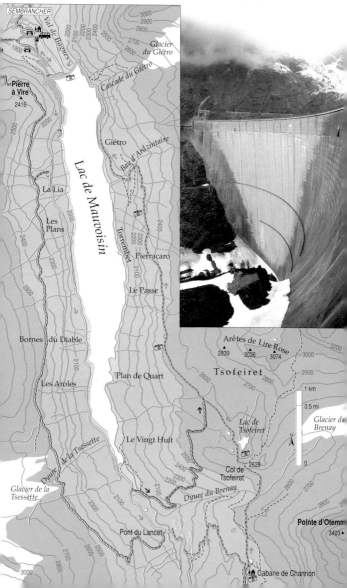

Walk 24 (Valais): LAC DE CLEUSON

Distance/time: 12km/7.5mi; 3h35min *using chairlift*

Best period: July-September

Grade: *easy if you take the chairlift,* with an ascent of about 250m/820ft and descent of 750m/2460ft; otherwise fairly strenuous (see under 'Transport' below); highest point 2358m, lowest 1733m

Equipment: hiking boots

Refreshments/accommodation: refreshments available in Siviez (also called Super-Nendaz), but none en route; accommodation in Super-Nendaz, Haute-Nendaz, Sion

Transport: 🚌 from Sion to Siviez (with a change at Haute-Nendaz, Jul-Sep, about 4-5 times/day, journey time over 1h). 🚗: from Sierre take exit 27 (Sion-Est) off the A9 motorway; from Martigny, take exit 25 off the A9. Follow signs to Nendaz. Pass Basse-Nendaz and follow signs to Siviez, a modest ski resort in the proximity of world-famous Verbier (large car park). Then 🚠 chairlift to La Tsa (Jul/Aug *only*). *Outside Jul/Aug, you must climb from Siviez to Chervé (an extra 530m/1h30min of ascent).*

Shorter walk: Cleuson Dam (2h35min, ascent about 150m; descent 700m). Follow the main walk to the 1h05min-point, then descend straight to the lake. Cross the dam wall and pick up the main walk again at the 2h35min-point.

Alternative walk: Lac du Grand Désert (*adds* 1h10min up, 50min down and 320m of ascent). Follow the main walk to the 1h45min-point, then continue up the gravel road. You cross a stream and pass the Refuge de St-Laurent (2485m, Jul-Sep, 32 dormitory places, ☎ 027 288 50 05). Continue on

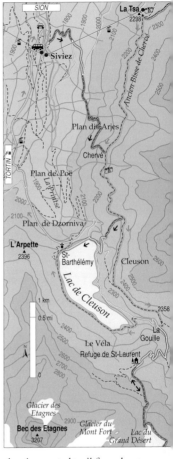

the signposted trail from here up to the Lac du Grand Désert (2642m) in a stark landscape — a sharp contrast to the flower-filled pastures below.

Tip: For a magnificent view of the Alps, take the chairlift from Siviez to Tortin (2050m), then cable car to the Col des Gentianes (2894m) and finally another cable car up to Mont Fort (3328m). In the summer, the tourist office in Nendaz offers early-bird trips to Mont Fort (departure before 5am) for a spectacular sunrise.

151

Approaching the Lac de Cleuson beyond La Gouille

This is a pleasant and easy walk — at least in July and August, when the chairlift operates. You'll be traversing one of the lesser-known valleys in the Valais, full of wild flowers and shrubs, and circling a turquoise lake in the midst of splendid Alpine scenery.

Take the chairlift from the BASE STATION in **Siviez** (1733m) to **La Tsa** (2338m). Follow the gently undulating path along the old **Bisse de Chervé**; unfortunately, only remnants of this old irrigation channel are visible today (wooden supports in a rock face; **25min**).

You pass the signposted **Chervé** junction (2260m, **40min**) and shortly thereafter get a first glimpse of Lake Cleuson. Go straight over the next signposted junction (2321m, **1h05min**), keeping to the high-level path. *(But turn down right here, if you are doing the Shorter walk.)*

The path runs parallel with the **Lac de Cleuson**, about 150m in height above it. At a junction simply signposted CHEMIN PÉDESTRE, bear right (the faint trail straight on doesn't lead 152

anywhere). You then pass the signpost **La Gouille** (2323m, **1h45min**) and reach a motorable gravel road. *(The Alternative walk heads up this road, past a mountain hut.)*

Turn right and walk down the road until you are almost at the southern tip of the lake, then turn sharp left *(no signpost; 2258m, 1h55min)*. Go around the lake anti-clockwise until you reach the chapel of **St-Barthélémy** at the northwestern tip of the lake (2187m, **2h35min**). *(The Shorter walk comes in from the dam wall here.)*

Don't cross the DAM; descend the waymarked path just a few metres from the chapel. When you are level with the base of the dam wall, turn left and follow the gravel road back to **Siviez** (**3h35min**).

Walk 25 (Valais): GRANDE DIXENCE DAM

See also photograph page 47
Distance/time: 8km/5mi;
3h15min *by cable car*
Best period: July-September
Grade: moderate-strenuous,
with an ascent of 510m/
1675ft; highest point 2804m,
lowest 2365m
Equipment: hiking boots,
warm clothing (you are at
almost 3000m altitude)
Refreshments/accommoda-tion: Hôtel du Barrage at the
foot of the dam (the former
housing for dam workers,
(027 281 13 22, www.hotel-
barrage.ch); Cabane de Prafleuri (open Jul-Sep; 59 places;
(027 281 17 80); Cabane des
Ecoulaies ((027 281 21 54)
Transport: 🚌 from the bus
station in Sion (next to the
railway station) to Le Chargeur (runs about every two
hours in summer, journey time
1h15min). 🚗: A9 motorway
to Sion Est, then follow signs
towards Val d'Hérens. In Vex
turn right into the Val d'Hérémence and drive to Le Chargeur at the head of the valley,
below the Grande Dixence
Dam (2141m, parking areas).
Le Chargeur consists of a hotel
with restaurant, a kiosk, an
information centre and the
valley station of the cable car.
The 🚡 runs up to the crest of
the dam (09.30-18.20 Jul/Aug,
10.00-17.20 Jun/Sep/Oct).
Add 45min if, instead of taking

the cable car, you walk up to
the dam (add 250m of ascent),
and 25min if you walk down.
Shorter walk: Lac des Dix.
Just follow the lakeside path as
long as you like.
Longer walk: Mont Blava
(4h05min, ascent 640m). You
must be sure-footed and have a
head for heights. Follow the
main walk to the 1h45min-
point, then take the trail (*not*
the level path) to your left,
rising along the ridge to the
top of **Mont Blava** (2932m).
Return the same way.
Tip: The galleries inside the
dam can be visited on a 1km-
long guided tour lasting about
an hour. Wear warm clothing;
it's only about 6°C/43°F inside
the dam. See www.grande-
dixence.ch.

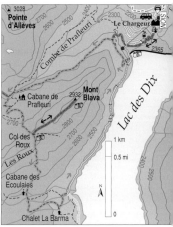

D riving up the Val d'Hérémence, you suddenly see
an immense structure at the head of the valley —
the Barrage de la Grande Dixence. The Grande Dixence
is one of the world's highest dams. From its base you
stare up at this 285m-high wall of concrete in disbelief.
If you do the longer walk to the top of Mont Blava, the
view from the peak lets you take in the true dimensions
of the Lac des Dix, the artificial lake held back by the
dam, set amidst delightful Alpine scenery.

Left: the construction of a large dam is always accompanied by the building of a chapel.
Below left: view over the Lac des Dix from the Col des Roux

ravine (**Combe de Prafleuri**). The trail ascends through this ravine to the **Cabane de Prafleuri** (2624m, **1h15min**). (*Note:* because of recent rock fall, construction work to slightly reroute the trail will take place in the summer of 2009.)

Continue the ascent towards the COL DES ROUX on a path through rocks and boulders. Whereas your views have been confined so far by the rocky mountain slopes, once you reach the **Col des Roux** (2804m, **1h45min**) all of a sudden the curtain is drawn and the Lac des Dix is at your feet.

(If you wish to improve on this already-gorgeous view, the Longer walk would take you to the peak of Mont Blava at 2932m — an additional 30min up, 20min down).

Descending from the **Col des Roux**, you pass close to an isolated hut (**Cabane des Ecoulaies**, 2575m, **2h10min**) and arrive at the **Chalet La Barma** (2458m, **2h30min**). The path turns left just before the chalet and reaches the gravel road beside the lake.

Follow this road — traversing about half a dozen tunnels, one of which is over 300m long and illuminated — back to the DAM WALL (**3h15min**). Then either take the cable car down to **Le Chargeur**, or walk down the zigzag path, passing the chapel shown above.

The upper station of the cable car (2437m) from **Le Chargeur** (2141m) is higher than the top of the dam (2365m). Walk down the wide path alongside the lake, past the TOP OF THE DAM WALL. Then, 130m past the crest, turn sharp right at the sign-posted junction for PRAFLEURI. After a few switchbacks you enter a sparsely-vegetated

Walk 26 (Valais): BISSE DU RO

Distance/time: 8km/5mi; 2h (1h each way)
Best period: June to October
Grade: easy ascent/descent of only about 200m/650ft, but you must be sure-footed and have a very good head for heights! Many stretches along this walk are *very* exposed (although usually secured). Take care not to bang your head on low, overhanging rocks. In the spring or after heavy rainfall the trail may be closed; *please heed the corresponding warning signs.* Highest point 1662m, lowest 1578m
Equipment: hiking boots
Refreshments/accommodations: none en route. Accommodation in Crans, Montana, and Sierre
Transport: the starting point is Plans-Mayens, a wide-spread settlement of holiday apartments north of Crans-sur-Sierre. The three villages Crans-sur-Sierre, Montana and Aminona form a world-famous glitzy resort known as Crans-Montana, on a sunny plateau above Sierre. Crans and Montana sprawl for more than 3km from east to west. 🚌 from Sierre or Sion to Crans-Montana (excellent connections, as follows; for timetables see www.cie-smc.ch or www.sbb.ch): (1) 🚌 from Sierre via Mollens to the Vignettes bus stop at Montana; (2) 🚌 from Sierre via Chermignon to the TéléCrans bus stop at Crans; (3) 🚌 from Sierre to Sion, then 🚌 to the Pas de l'Ours bus stop in Crans; (4) 🚟 funicular from Sierre (the station is a couple of minutes' walk from the Sierre railway station) to the Vermala bus stop in the eastern part of Montana (a 4.2km-long ride), then walk to the Vignettes bus stop. For (1)-(4) then onward 🚌 to Plans-Mayens (3-4 times/day, free of charge). (Once you reach the resort of Crans/Montana/Aminona, all bus transport is free.)

🚗: drive from Sierre via Chermignon to Crans, then take the signposted road up to Plans-Mayens from the triangular Hôtel de l'Etrier. After 2.0km there is a designated parking area on the left at 1626m. Or walk up: follow the road, but take the signposted short-cut off the third hairpin bend.

The most spectacular and daring of all ancient water irrigation channels in the Valais, the Bisse du Ro vividly illustrates the desperation of people needing water for their fields and vineyards. And what a contrast to the audacious dams constructed in recent times such

As you head up the Bisse du Ro, the Tseuzier Dam can be seen at the head of the valley.

as the Tseuzier Dam up the valley which can be spotted from the Bisse du Ro. Built in the 14th century, the Bisse du Ro was operational until 1947. An octogenarian couple I once met there told me (as we sipped local wine on a bench beside the trail) how they used to play as children along the *bisse* — which was totally unprotected at that time. Today, wooden and concrete boardwalks with handrails protect the walker.

From the parking area in **Plans-Mayens** (1626m), follow signposting for BISSE DU RO, descending 50m through forest. When you reach the old water channel (**Bisse du Ro**), turn right. The path alternates between very exposed stretches (see right) and leisurely, broad forest trails. The channel only carries water along short stretches (for tourists). In and out of ravines with brittle rock, you reach a signposted junction with a CROSS and a BENCH (1662m, **1h**).
Retrace your steps from here to **Plans-Mayens** (**2h**).

At the most exposed points, there are sturdy protective handrails

156

Walk 27 (Valais): ROC DE LA VACHE

Distance/time: 12.2km/8mi; 5h15min

Best period: end of June until October

Grade: strenuous, with an ascent of 990m/3250ft (highest point 2581m, lowest 1667m); the trails are good

Equipment: hiking boots

Refreshments/accommodation: none en route. Plenty of accommodation facilities in Zinal

Transport: 🚆 to Sierre, then post 🚐 from Sierre to Zinal (change in Vissoie, about 6-7 buses a day, journey time 1h). 🚗: exit 29 off the A9 motorway (Sierre Est). First follow signposting to Val d'Anniviers, then follow signs for Ayer and Zinal. It's a drive of 30km (30min) from Sierre, all well signposted. Roads are cleared all year round. Numerous and free parking places in Zinal.

Alternative walk: Tracuit hut (4h45min *one way*, ascent 1580m, straightforward but strenuous and long). Follow the main walk to the junction at the 2h30min-point. Go left at this junction and follow the waymarked path for another 2h15min, to the Tracuit hut (3256m, 110 dormitory places, staffed from July to mid-September, ☎ 027 475 15 00). This is a splendid location, with gorgeous views. Return the same way, allowing about 3h to descend.

Zinal is a year-round holiday resort at the end of the Val d'Anniviers, nuzzled up against magnificent 4000m-high mountain peaks — Weisshorn (4506m), Zinalrothorn (4221m), Ober Gabelhorn (4063m) and Dent Blanche (4357m). The resort boasts some 300km of hiking trails. Streams, cascades, tarns, passes, Alpine huts, varied vegetation and heavenly mountain scenery — it all comes together on this marvel of a walk.

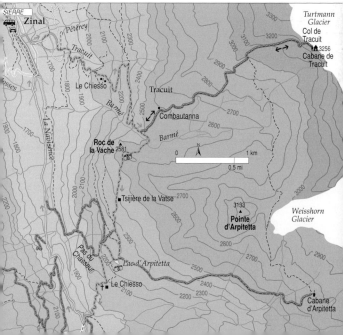

From the VILLAGE SIGN (1667m) at the southern end of **Zinal** turn 90° left and follow the road 100m uphill to the HOTEL LES BOUQUETINS. Turn right (waymarking starts here), then go left after 150m and keep left again after a further 30m. You are now on a gravel track. After another 150m turn left on a path that zigzags for about three minutes up to the surfaced road you left earlier. Follow the road through a hairpin bend to the right. After about 250m, the surface runs out and the road becomes an earthen track. Where it hairpins to the left, walk straight ahead for 100m, then take the narrow hiking path (TRACUIT painted on a rock; **20min**). Ignore a path off to the right immediately. The path snakes up past a couple of Alpine huts (**Le Chiesso,** 2061m, **1h15min**). After a couple of wide switch-

backs, the path winds up beside a stream, the **Torrent du Barmé**, and reaches a junction on a PLATEAU (2477m, **2h30min**), where you turn right. *(But for the Alternative walk, go left.)* Cross the *torrent* and, after a short, final ascent, reach the highest point of the walk — the saddle just below the summit of **Roc de la Vache** (2581m, **2h50min**) — a great picnic spot.

The descent path heads south through Alpine meadows, passes a somewhat ramshackle but idyllic hut (**Tsijière de la Vatse**, 2388m, **3h10min**) and reaches a tarn, the **Lac d'Arpitetta** (2230m, **3h30min**) in a most picturesque setting. A path branches off left here to another Alpine hut (Cabane d'Arpitetta, 2766m), but take the path to the right. This heads north for 300m, then bends back south. At a junction (2161m, **3h40min**) *don't*

Lac d'Arpitetta (left); walkers heading from the Roc de la Vache towards the Lac d'Arpitetta, with the snow- and ice-covered Zinal-rothorn and Weisshorn to the left (below left); footbridge at the confluence of streams at the southernmost point of the walk (below right)

take the Pas du Chasseur which forks off to the right (marked *'difficile'*), but continue straight ahead through Alpine rose, juniper and larch to another landfall with the name **Le Chiesso** (hut, cross, 2082m, **3h45min**).

The path now zigzags down to the impressive CONFLUENCE OF STREAMS draining the Zinal, Weisshorn and Moming glaciers. You cross a footbridge and reach a gravel road (1908m, **4h10min**). Turn right (the Cabane du Petit Mountet is signposted to the left) and follow the road back to **Zinal** (**5h15min**).

HIKING IN ZERMATT

Zermatt (1605m) is Zermatt. *Don't* compromise and stay somewhere else in the valley. With 400km of marked paths, Zermatt itself offers you the following five hiking areas: Zermatt and its close surroundings; Rothorn to the northeast; Monte Rosa to the southeast; Matterhorn to the southwest; and the Höhbalmen, Arben and Schweifinen area to the west. Only in the last of this list are there no mechanical aids to facilitate the ascent; the others are accessible via cable cars or funiculars. A sixth area could even be added — the lower-lying Matter Valley, with the villages of Täsch, Randa, St Niklaus and Grächen. In addition to Walks 28 and 29, here is a potpourri of suggested walks, some easy, some tough. The Zermatt Tourist Office *Wanderkarte* (hiking map; 1:25,000) covers areas 1-5.

Zermatt to Zmutt and back

(2h30min, ascent/descent 330m, map overleaf). This is one of the loveliest (and busiest) walks in Zermatt and a great way to start your stay in Matterhorn country. It's as easy as pie, with wide gravel paths, a gentle ascent, numerous benches, and with the best-known side of the Matterhorn always in view. Walk to the southernmost point in Zermatt and bear right for ZMUTT. Climb through pastures and larches to a first group of chalets (1900m), to reach **Zmutt** (1936m; refreshments). Instead of returning the same way, take the delightful trail via the hamlet of **Herbrigg**: retrace your steps for five minutes, to the chalets at 1900m and turn left (we go a shorter way to Zermatt than the '2h' indicated on the sign). Then go right after a few metres and, at the junction after another 50m, go right again. Ten minutes later there is a 50m stretch of path with a handrail, but the trail is easy.

Oberrothorn is about as high as you can go in the Alps without climbing equipment (3414m). It offers a fantastic panorama. The paths are good, with no particular difficulties. Despite its altitude, the summit is normally snow-free in summer. Nevertheless, be sure to bring all the necessary equipment (see page 68) with you, in particular warm clothing (the temperature can easily drop below 0°C, and precipitation falls as snow even if it feels tropical in Zermatt!). Don't do this walk on your first day in Zermatt; do a couple of hikes at lower altitude first to adjust to the higher altitudes. Most people take the funicular and two cable cars to Unterrothorn, but if you are in shape you can walk up from Zermatt (ascent 1800m), for instance via Findeln.

Ascent to Oberrothorn

(1h45min, ascent 430m). Take the � funicular in Zermatt to Sunnegga (the valley station is directly opposite the Gornergrat railway on the other side of the Mattervispa, the stream that runs through Zermatt), then the 🚡 cable cars — first to Blauherd and from there to

160

Zmutt, where you can get refreshments before walking down to Zermatt

Unterrothorn. From the **Unterrothorn** STATION (3103m) descend eastwards across the wide ridge to **Furggji** (2981m, **20min**). The wounds of winter tourism are unfortunately all too obvious in the area around Unterrothorn. Continue eastwards, now gaining height, first slowly, then more sharply as the path zigzags its way around the southeastern ridge of **Oberrothorn** (3414m).

Descent from Oberrothorn

Besides retracing your steps to the Unterrothorn station and using the cable cars, there are alternatives.

1 (2h, descent 850m). Retrace your steps to **Furggji** and turn left (southwards) to the **Fluealp hut** (2618m, restaurant and accommodation, ☏ 027 967 2551). Turn west, pass pretty **Lake Stelli**, and continue to **Blauherd** (2571m); return via 🛏 and 🚠. (If you want to keep walking, from Blauherd you can descend the path to Sunnegga and from there walk on to Zermatt — either via Tufteren or Winkelmatten.)

2 (4h15min, descent 1800m). As (1) above to **Lake Stelli**, but then descend via the picturesque settlement of **Findeln** (2051m, photo opportunities galore with the Matterhorn as backdrop). Then follow the signs to Zermatt via **Winkelmatten**.

3 (3h45min, descent 1800m). As (1) above to **Furggji**, then turn right (north) and descend the high valley called **Tufterchumme** (on a path full of edelweiss) via **Tufteren** (2215m) and **Tiefenmatten** (1872m) to Zermatt.

Platthorn (9h, very strenuous ascent of 1750m). Platthorn is almost as high as Oberrothorn on the opposite site of the valley. Like Oberrothorn, it offers grandiose views, but because there is no mechanical help, you have to earn them all yourself, starting in Zermatt. Follow Walk 28 to the **Trift hut** (2h15min; an overnight stay is recommended). Turn right (north) here and follow the path into the valley for about 600m, then turn right at **Vieliboden** (2453m). Climb the high valley **Triftchumme** (sometimes over old snowfields) to the **Platthorn** SUMMIT (3345m, **5h30min**). Return the same way to Zermatt (3h30min).
*(Neighboring **Mettelhorn** at 3406m involves an additional 30min of ascent, but should only be tackled by those with the proper equipment and glacier experience. Cross only if the crevasses are clearly visible, to avoid dangerous areas. Ask at the Trift hut about conditions on the glacier.)*

Europaweg from Gasenried to Zermatt (30km, 12-13h).

Inaugurated in 1997, the 'Europe Path' offers fantastic views on the approach to Zermatt. A long, demanding walk, only suitable for experienced mountain hikers and best broken into two or three days; see www.europaweg.ch.

161

Walk 28 (Valais): HÖHBALMEN RIDGE PATH

Distance/time: 18km/11.2mi; 6h45min

Best period: June to October

Grade: strenuous, with an ascent of 1170m/3840ft, but technically easy. Highest point 2741m, lowest 1605m

Equipment: hiking boots

Refreshments/accommodation: Pension Edelweiss (open from early June until early Oct, 4 rooms (10 beds), ℂ 027 967 22 36); Berggasthaus Trift (open end of Jun until end of Sep, 5 rooms (16 beds) and dormitory with 20 places, ℂ 079 408 70 20 (mobile), www.zermatt.ch/trift

Transport: 🚆 to Visp, then 🚌 from Visp to Zermatt (see page 56). 🚗: Zermatt is car-free; only bicycles, electrically-powered cars, horse-drawn sleighs and carriages are allowed. There are 900 open-air and 2900 covered places in car parks in the village of Täsch, 5km from Zermatt. Some car parks operate a taxi service to Zermatt. Shuttle trains between Täsch and Zermatt run every 20min.

Shorter walks

1 Zermatt • Zmutt • Zermatt (2h30min, ascent/descent 330m, easy). See page 160.

2 Zermatt • Höhbalmen • Zermatt (5h15min, ascent/descent 1060m). Follow the main walk to the Höhbalmen junction (2665m, 3h30min). Here you can descend a steep path back to Zermatt — either via Alterhaupt/Edelweiss or via Hubel (both eventually link up with your outgoing route).

Alternative walk: Schönbiel hut (9h30min, additional ascent/descent of about 400m, *not on our map, but unmissable, with no forks*). This hut, west of the main walk, can be reached in 1h30min from the junction (2327m) at the 4h30min-point. Those who are really fit can do it all in one day, but why not make a 2-3 day trip out of it, staying overnight at Trift hut and then the Schön-biel hut (2694m, open end Mar until mid-May and end Jun until mid-Sep, dormitory with 80 places, ℂ 027 967 13 54). *For a map, see page 160.*

Matterhorn — magical, mysterious, miraculous, marvellous, magnificent, moving. The Höhbalmen ridge path is a classic walk with breathtaking views over the whole of the Zermatt Valley, from the Mischabel range as far as the Monte Rosa and Breithorn massifs, with the famous Matterhorn north face staring you straight in the face. As on the north face of the Eiger, fame and tragedy go hand-in-hand on the Matterhorn. One of Zermatt's mountain guides became a celebrity: Ulrich Inderbinen (1900-2004), who was still climbing the Matterhorn at the age of 90. His grave is in Zermatt's cemetery.

From the **Zermatt** RAILWAY STATION, walk into the centre along the main road (BAHNHOFSTRASSE), to pass the CHURCH (**7min**). The MATTERHORN MUSEUM next to it is housed underground. Among much else, you would learn that Sir Winston Churchill climbed Monte Rosa/Dufourspitze and President Theodore Roosevelt the Matterhorn. The website (www.zermatt.ch/e/matterhornmuseum) also offers a large-scale downloadable plan of the resort). At a walkers' signpost 100m past the church, leave Bahnhofstrasse for EDELWEISS/TRIFT,

turning right into an alley (SCHÄLPMATTGASSE). Leave the houses of Zermatt behind you, and turn right at a junction (where the trail to the left is signposted to Herbrigg). Crossing meadow slopes, you enter the **Trift Gorge**. The trail snakes steeply uphill to the ALTERHAUPT HOTEL (PENSION EDELWEISS; 1961m, **1h**). Continue the ascent through the gorge, to emerge at the TRIFT MOUNTAIN HUT (2337m, **2h15min**) at the base of a *cirque*. One last effort has to be made now, to reach the balcony path on the Höhbalmen ridge: from the Trift hut, keep

The Matterhorn from Zermatt (above) and from the Höhbalmen ridge path (left)

left, cross the **Trift** stream and climb in switchbacks to a junction on **Höhbalmen** (2665m, **3h30min**), where the Matterhorn comes into view.

The *RIDGE TRAIL* now traverses Höhbalmen's vast Alpine meadows. After reaching the highest point of this walk, a place called **Schwarzläger** (2741m; no particular landmark), you descend — first gently, then more steeply — to the next signposted junction (2327m, **4h30**). *(The Alternative walk turns right here.)* Turn left and follow the path at the left of the stream (**Zmutt-bach**) via **Chalbermatten** to the hamlet of **Zmutt** (**5h45min**) and from there back to **Zermatt** (6h45min).

Distance/time: 3.5km/2.2mi; 1h45min

Best period: July to October

Grade: easy ascent of 200m/650ft and descent of 480m/1575ft, but you must be sure-footed. Highest point 3135m, lowest 2695m

Equipment: hiking boots

Refreshments/accommodation: At 3100m, the Kulmhotel Gornergrat is the highest hotel in the Swiss Alps, surrounded by 29 peaks of over 4000m in height (☎ 027 966 64 00, www.matterhorngroup.ch/en/gornergrat, also www.gornergrat.ch).

Transport: 🚆 to Zermatt (see page 56), then 🚠 cog railway to Gornergrat station (3085m, journey time 38min). Return on the same railway line, from Rotenboden station.

Tip: There are also sunrise trips to Gornergrat from mid-Jun to mid-Sep (Thu only).

Alternative walks

1 Lower Gornergrat slopes (1h45min-2h15min, descent/ascent 230m, easy). If you visit Zermatt in June, there will still be snow on the Gornergrat ridge. But the first part of the trail towards the Monte Rosa hut is likely to be snow-free. So start off from the Rotenboden railway station and do an out-and-back traverse along the lower Gornergrat slopes (the main walk in reverse) — going either as far as the descending path from the ridge (2695m), or a bit further — to see the glacier and some ibex up close (see overleaf).

2 Glacier walk. The path used in Alternative walk 1 above continues across the glacier to the Monte Rosa hut. It is way-marked, but do not attempt it unless you have the relevant experience on glaciers. Guided tours across the glacier are on offer from Jul to mid-Sep once a week (☎ 027 966 24 60).

3) Zermatt — Gornergrat — Zermatt (depending on the route, 5-6h for the ascent of about 1550m, 3h30min-5h for the descent). The very fit could climb to the Gornergrat summit and return to Zermatt in one day, but this is a very strenuous walk. Why not make a two-day trip out of it and enjoy a night at the Kulmhotel in magnificent surroundings — or use the Gornergrat railway to shorten the walk. The trains stop at Findelbach (1770m), Riffelalp (2211m), Riffelberg (2582m), Rotenboden (2815m) and Gornergrat (3085m). You can get off the train at any station and board again later in the day with the same ticket.

a) One possible ascent is via the hamlet Winkelmatten and Riffelalp to Riffelberg and from there either left or right along the railway tracks to Gornergrat. For the descent follow the main walk from Gornergrat to Rotenboden, then past the idyllic Riffelsee (2775m). Continue, always with the Matterhorn in view, via Gagenhaupt (2564m), from where you could return to Riffelberg and Riffelalp. Otherwise continue the descent via the Furi 🚠 to Zermatt.

b) Instead of taking the Gornergrat railway, you can ease part of the ascent by taking the 🚠 to Furi. From the mountain station of the cable car, follow the road towards Zermatt, cross a stream and, a few metres further on, fork right to Riffelalp. Continue via Riffelberg to the Gornergrat summit.

Topping 4500m: Mount Liskamm

Gornergrat is Zermatt's most popular destination, offering one of the most famous, awe-inspiring and humbling vistas in the Alps — if not the world. About two-thirds of Swiss mountains above 4000m are almost within reach from Gornergrat — from the gigantic icy masses of the Monte Rosa massif just

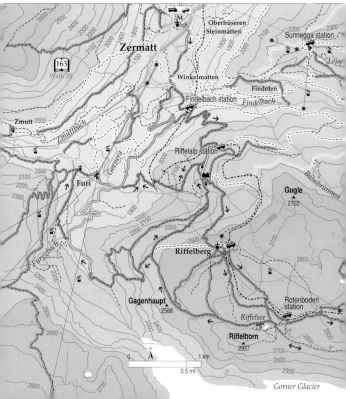

Gorner Glacier

opposite in the south or the Matterhorn to the west.

The Gornergrat cog railway makes it easy for everyone to enjoy the spectacle. However, there are a great many ways to make one's own way up to the summit on foot, and the railway can always be used if you feel like shortening your walk. Why not spend a night at the Kulmhotel on the top of Gornergrat at 3100m: where else could you enjoy in such comfort the majestic play of light and shade, as the sun rises and sets over those icy crowns?

The main walk described below is easy if you are surefooted, but several variations for the more physically fit are suggested on page 165 and shown on the map.

From the **Gornergrat** RAILWAY STATION walk past the KULM-HOTEL to the highest point of the OBSERVATION PLATFORM (3135m, **5min**). Behind the walled-in area, take the trail signposted MONTE-ROSA-HÜTTE, heading east along the ridge. After 500m (3095m, **15min**), fork right and zigzag down a steep, narrow path (*not* waymarked).

After you have dropped 400m in height, you reach the TRAIL TO THE MONTE ROSA HUT at a T-junction (2695m, **55min**). You can spot the hut — it's about 2.5km south-southeast across the glacier, on the moraine. (You might like to walk a bit closer to the glacier from this point — and watch a herd of ibex *(allow an extra 30-40min out and back)*. If so, turn left at the T-junction. After five minutes, keep straight on at the next junction (2658m), where the trail goes right towards the Monte Rosa hut. Go on for another 10-15 minutes, then return.)

Turn right at the T-junction at the 55min-point (or walk straight ahead if you have been to see the glacier). Now you traverse the slopes of Gornergrat, gently climbing, all the way to the **Rotenboden** RAILWAY STATION (2815m, **1h45min**). Don't miss the lake just below the station (**Riffel-see**, 2775m) — it's a popular spot for calendar pictures, with the Matterhorn as a backdrop.

Top left: the path to Rotenboden station on the Gornergrat slopes. Bottom left: it's quite likely that you will encounter a herd of ibex.

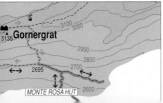

Walk 30 (Valais): MÄLLIG AND GEBIDUM

Distance/time: 9km/5.6mi; 3h40min (see also Shorter walks)

Best period: June to October

Grade: moderate-strenuous, with an ascent of 450m/1475ft and descent of 1000m/3300ft (highest point 2764m, lowest 1800m). Technically easy, but you must be sure-footed.

Equipment: hiking boots

Refreshments/accommodation: Restaurant Hannigalp at the mountain station of the gondola; none en route. Plenty of accommodation in Saas Fee

Transport: 🚐 to Visp, then change to post 🚌 to Saas Fee (connections every 30min). 🚗: drive along the Rhône Valley to the town of Visp, then fork off for Saas Fee. Saas Fee is car-free; there are large car parks at the village entrance. All hotels and some holiday apartments offer free transport from the parking area.

Shorter walks

1 Hannigalp — Schönegge — Saas Fee (1h50min, ascent 150m, descent 680m). This is a very easy walk in breath-taking surroundings. Take the 🚠 gondola up to Hannigalp. Out of the top station, turn left (southwest); the trail goes down gently and crosses the streams Torrenbach (2283m) and Triftbach (2300m). Immediately after the latter, bear right and climb to a junction. This place is called Schönegge ('Beautiful Corner', 2419m). *Nomen est omen* indeed — the 4000m summits and their glaciers seem almost within arm's length from here. Take the zigzag trail down to Saas Fee — against a great backdrop.

2 Saas Fee — Schönegge — Hannigalp (2h30min, ascent

680m, descent 150m). This is Shorter walk 1 in reverse, for those looking to work up a little sweat. From Hannigalp take the 🚠 gondola back to Saas Fee — or walk down (1h15min by the shortest signposted route).

Alternative walks *(appropriate map needed for both)*
1 Britannia Hut and Klein Allalin. There are different ways to approach this walk, south of Saas Fee. (a) The shortest (about 1h45min, ascent 90m) is to take the 🚠 cable car up to Felskinn (2989m), from where a wide trail crosses snow via the small Chessjen Glacier (this should not pose a problem — you can cross it with hiking boots) to the large Britannia hut (3030m, 134 places, booking essential, (027 957 22 88, www.britannia.ch). Allow 45min to the hut, then climb

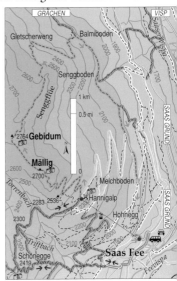

Klein Allalin (3070m) in just a few minutes, for a view down to the Mattmark Dam and up to towering snow- and ice-covered peaks. (b) A popular route, which should only be undertaken if you have a head for heights, is to take the 🚠 gondola from Saas Fee to Plattjen (2570m) and then follow the well-marked high-level trail to the Britannia Hut (2h, ascent 500m). Then return to Saas Fee via the trail in (a) above.
2 Allalinhorn (4h return, ascent 500m, guided, details from the tourist office). If you ever wanted to stand on a 4000m-high peak without too much effort, Allalinhorn (4027m) gives you the oppor-tunity. Cable cars and the Metro Alpin take you up to 3454m. From there it's a short (2h) guided climb across the snow fields.

Alternative walk 1(b): if you don't take the gondola from Saas Fee to Plattjen, you can walk up via this trail.

A sea of Alpine roses between Balmiboden and Senggboden

Saas Fee — pearl of the Alps. Lying in a valley next door to Zermatt, Saas Fee is quieter than its world-famous neighbor. But the Mischabel Range which curves around Saas Fee like a clam enclosing a pearl offers a dozen 4000m-high peaks and makes this glacial *cirque* a unique landscape in the Alps. Mount Mällig is arguably the best viewpoint from which to admire the 4000m summits which surround Saas Fee.

Take the gondola from **Saas Fee** to **Hannigalp** (2336m) — or walk up (Shorter walk 2). A few metres from the Hannigalp station an initially broad path with large switchbacks leads you up to the summit of **Mällig** (2700m, also spelled Mellig, **1h**) — a great place for a picnic. The trail continues among rocks to the highest point of this circuit, the top of **Gebidum** (2764m, **1h20min**), from where you can also enjoy a view to the Bernese Alps in the distance.

From here the trail descends on the slopes of **Senggflüe**, soon turning left (2604m, **1h45min**). At **Gletscherweng** (the Bider glacier once extended down to here) the path swings right. At spot height 2274m there is another sharp left-turn, and after steep

170

switchbacks you meet the high-level trail between Grächen and Saas Fee at **Balmiboden** (2120m, **2h35min**).
Turn right and walk through beautiful forest. At the junction 10 minutes later (*SIGNPOST:* **Senggboden**) bear right, and a few minutes later reach another **Senggboden** sign (2045m). Keep right for *MELCHBODEN* at the next signposted junction. The path joins the unsurfaced road up to Hannigalp on a hairpin bend (2008m). Follow this downhill for a couple of minutes, then bear left on a footpath, down to a *TARN* on your right (*SIGNPOST:* **Melchbode**, 1940m, **3h15min**). Rejoining the waymarked road, follow it round a hairpin bend, towards *HOHNEGG*, soon arriving back in **Saas Fee** (1800m, **3h40min**).

Walk 31 (Valais): LÖTSCHEN VALLEY RIDGE PATH

See also photograph page 55
Distance/time: 20km/12.4mi, 6h20min from Fafleralp to Ferden (see also Shorter walks below)

Best period: June to October

Grade: easy-moderate, but long, with an ascent of 740m/2430ft and descent of 1140m/3740ft; highest point 2100m, lowest 1370m

Equipment: hiking boots

Refreshments/accommodation: In the valley, there are numerous possibilities in the Lötschental villages of Ferden, Kippel, Wiler and Blatten. On the ridge path, Hotel Fafleralp is located near the start of the trail (℅ 027 939 14 51, www.fafleralp.ch); high up in Lauchernalp are three possibilities: Berghaus Lauchernalp (dormitories and rooms, ℅ 027 939 12 50); Alpenhotel Zur Wildi (open Jul-Oct, ℅ 027 939

Alternative walk 2: the Lonza stream, with a view to Lang Glacier. This amount of snow (in May) means that it is too early for walking.

19 89, www.zur-wildi.ch); Ferienpark Alpine Village (a 'holiday park' with 2-3 bedroom apartments, ℂ 027 938 82 00, www.alpinevillage. ch). Refreshments are available in numerous Alpine hamlets on the ridge path. The Lötschental tourist office is in Wiler: ℂ 027 938 88 88; www.loetschental. ch; www.lauchernalp.ch

Transport:  to Goppenstein at the southern end of the Lötschberg Tunnel, then post  from Goppenstein to the Lötschental villages (runs hourly; from Jun-Oct the bus continues up to Fafleralp, terminating at the large car park at Gletscherstafel. Last bus from Fafleralp at 19.18 via Ferden (19.42) to Goppenstein (19.50); last bus from Ferden at 18.10 to Fafleralp (18.38). 🚗: From cantonal road 9 in the Rhône Valley, turn north between Sierre and Visp following signposting to 'Lötschberg, Gampel'. From the Bernese Oberland take the Lötschberg Tunnel from Kandersteg to Goppenstein (car railway). There is a small covered car park in Ferden, a

car park at Wiler's cable car station, and a large parking area at Gletscherstafel near Fafleralp, where the main walk begins.

Shorter walks

1 Lötschen valley ridge path, eastern section (9km, 2h30min, ascent 200m, descent 400m). Take the 🚠 cable car from Wiler up to **Lauchernalp** STATION (1969m), then do this part of the main walk in reverse: follow the trail east via **Weritzalp** (2099m) and **Tellisalp** (1865m) to **Fafleralp** (1787m). Return by  to Wiler, if you left a car there, or back to base. If you do this stretch in the direction of the main walk (3h, ascent 400m, descent 200m), return by 🚠 cable car from Lauchernalp to Wiler, then by .

2 Lötschen valley ridge path, western section (11km, 3h45min, ascent 343m, descent 950m). Take the 🚠 cable car from Wiler up to **Lauchernalp** STATION (1969m), then pick up the main walk at the 2h35min-point and follow it to the end.

Tiny Lake Guggi (Guggisee; Alternative walk 2)

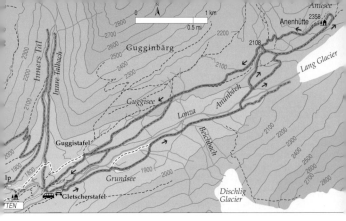

Alternative walks

1 Ridge path from Jeizinen to Faldumalp

(3h30min, ascent 850m, descent 230m, *not shown on our map*). This is a lesser-known ridge path above the outer Lötschen Valley. It starts in **Gampel** (635m), a village in the Rhône Valley. Take the 🚠 cable car in Gampel-Steg (operates all year round, more or less hourly from after 6.00 to almost 22.00) to the settlement of **Jeizinen** (1526m). Walk from Jeizinen to **Underi Fäsilalpu**, then **Fäsilalp** (1h30min) and from there to **Faldumalp** (3h30min). From Faldumalp use the map on page 176 to pick up the classic Lötschen Valley ridge path, making a two-day hike. *You will need a map for the first part.*

2 Gletscherstafel — Anen Hut — Gletscherstafel

(3h45min, ascent 600m, moderate). This really beautiful circuit starts at Gletscherstafel near Fafleralp (same starting point as the main walk, *see map above*). Highlights are the two tarns of Grundsee and Guggisee, reflecting the 3000m-high peaks; the awe-inspiring Langgletscher, marking the end of the Lötschental; and the larch woods, enchanting the walker with their golden autumnal hues. The trail leads to the Anen Hut (Anenhütte, 2358m, ☎ 027 939 17 64), from where the walk returns by a different route. From the **Gletscherstafel** CAR PARK walk east towards ANENHÜTTE, with the chalets and barns of Gletscherstafel on your left. In a few minutes you cross the **Lonza** stream, after which the trail turns left. Fifteen minutes from the bridge, don't miss the small path off right to the **Grundsee**. This path soon leads back to the main trail, where you continue through sparse larch woods. At a waymarked junction (**1h**), turn left, cross a bridge over the Lonza, and turn right for the ascent to the hut.* From the **Anen Hut** (2358m, **2h15min**) descend to the tiny tarn, **Guggisee** (2007m, **3h10min**), having ignored a path off left just beforehand. When you reach the chalets of **Guggistafel** (**3h30min**), *leave* the waymarked route and bear left on a path which descends back to Gletscherstafel (**3h45min**).

*You can shorten the walk at this point by omitting the steepish ascent to the Anen Hut: continue straight on here, picking up the trail again on its return leg, at spot height 2108.

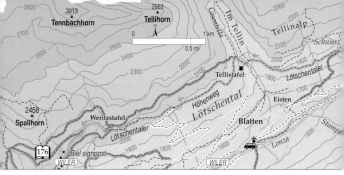

W hat a lovely and quiet gem — the Lötschen
Valley, the longest of the Valais valleys north of
the Rhône. Its four villages, Ferden, Kippel, Wiler and
Blatten are strung out like pearls. Meadows sprinkled
with tarns, barns and picturesque hamlets form the backdrop. Mountains, covered with small hanging glaciers,
tower up to 3000m — among them Bietschhorn (part
of the UNESCO World Natural Heritage Site encompassing Jungfrau, Aletsch and Bietschhorn). The head
of the valley is marked by the 'Long Glacier' (Langgletscher). Below it there are 200km of waymarked
paths, among them the famous Lötschentaler Höhen-
weg, a high-level walk that undulates through forests
and pastures on dirt roads, gravel roads and lovely trails.

The Lötschentaler Höhenweg comprises an eastern

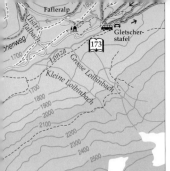

section (from Fafleralp to Lauchernalp via Tellistafel/ Tellialp and Weritzstafel/Weritzalp) and a western section (from Lauchernalp to Faldumalp via Kummenalp and Restialp). The two halves can be combined and/or walked in either direction. There are numerous ways to tailor this high-ridge path to your taste, and several paths leading down to valley villages allow you to shorten the walk. If you'd like to hike the path in its entire glory, either start at the head of the valley in Fafleralp and walk to Faldumalp, then down to Ferden (main description below), or vice versa. Many walkers take the cable car in Wiler (1419m, car park) to Lauchernalp (1969m) and then walk either the eastern or the western section. To return to your base, take the hourly post bus.

From the **Gletscherstafel** CAR PARK near Fafleralp, follow the sign LÖTSCHENTALER HÖHEN-WEG (1763m) and cross the meadow. After 100m, take either the road or the trail; both lead to the HOTEL FAFLER-ALP (1787m, **10min**). Next is the hamlet **Fafleralp** (1795m, lake, **15min**). From here take the dirt road gently uphill. Shortly after crossing the **Uistri** stream, bear left. You pass another lake (**Schwarzsee**, (1860m, **45min**) and arrive at the settlement **Tellistafel/ Tellialp** (1865m, **1h10min**, refreshments).

Bear right after the stream and start climbing (ignoring two paths off to the right some 10 minutes past Tellistafel). You

Colourful autumnal larches; above: signpost at the Hotel Fafleralp

pass the tiny LAKE shown below (1975m, **1h35min**) and reach a junction (2028m, **1h45min**). Continue straight on, to the hamlet of **Weritzstafel/Weritz-alp** (2099m, **2h05min**). From a road takes you to a settlement of about a dozen chalets (SIGNPOST: **Biel**, 2020m, **2h15min**). *Don't* continue on the road, but walk a few metres past the signpost, then go straight ahead. You cross a stream on a wooden BRIDGE (**2h30min**) and head uphill, ignoring any faint paths to the left. When you meet another road (**2h35min**), follow it uphill. The scattered settlement of **Lauchernalp**, with the MOUNTAIN STATION OF THE CABLE CAR from Wiler, is on your left. Soon you'll see a small new CHURCH on your right, with the BERGGASTHAUS LAUCHERNALP behind it. From the SIGNPOST **Lauchern-alp/Stafel** (2106m, **2h45min**) walk towards HOCKENALP,

passing a handful of huts. Signs direct you across mea-dows (where the wounds of ski tourism are only too apparent) to the hamlet of **Hockenalp** (2048m, **2h55min**, chapel, refreshments). The next destination is Kum-menalp. From Hockenalp's chapel, walk downhill for about 250m, then *leave* the gravel road just before a hair-pin bend to the left: fork right, uphill *(not signposted or way-marked)*. After a few metres a trail from the right merges with your path: keep straight on. About 50m past a MEMO-RIAL (**3h05min**), waymarks direct you through pastures dotted with boulders. At a junction go straight ahead uphill, to arrive at **Kummen-alp** (2090m, **3h45min**). From the GASTHAUS KUMMEN-ALP (refreshments) follow the gravel road downhill. At the junction **Trockene Stiege** (SIGNPOST; 2020m, **4h**) keep right towards RESTIALP. At 2100m, **Restialp** (about ten chalets, **4h15min**) marks the highest point in the walk. Take the path climbing a few metres to the IMBISSECKE RESTIALP (refreshments at weekends if the weather is fine!). Continue towards FALDUMALP. There is a short passage with handrails (**4h40min**), but the trail is not a problem. **Faldum-alp** (2037m, about 20 chalets, chapel, **5h10min**) marks the end of the Lötschen Valley ridge path. Retrace your steps for a couple of minutes to the stream you just crossed and take the trail to the right just past the bridge *(no signpost)* to descend to **Ferden** (**6h20min**).

Tiny snow-bound lake between Tellistafel and Weritzstafel, in May — too early for the Höhenweg

Walk 32 (Valais): ALETSCH GLACIER (UNESCO WORLD HERITAGE SITE) AND EGGISHORN

Distance/time: 16km/10mi; 6h10min (see also Shorter walks below)

Best period: June to October

Grade: strenuous, although technically easy. Ascent 650m/2130ft, descent 1350m/4430ft; highest point 2927m, lowest 1980m

Equipment: hiking boots

Refreshments/accommodation: restaurant at the Bettmer Ridge mountain station; upper station of Eggishorn cable car; valley station of Eggishorn cable car (called Fischeralp Kühboden); Märjelen Hut (also called 'Gletscherstube', open beginning of Jul to mid-Oct, with dormitories, ℂ 027 971 47 83, www.gletscher stube.ch); numerous possibilities in Bettmeralp, see www.bettmeralp.ch)

Transport: The starting point is the sunny car-free village of Bettmeralp (1957m) high above the Rhône Valley. Bettmeralp can be reached by cable car from Betten valley station (with large car park). *Don't* drive up to the old village of Betten Dorf (1200m, about a third of the way up from Betten valley station to Bettmeralp), because parking places are very scarce. 🚆 to Brig (direct from Geneva, Zurich, Basel and Berne). In Brig change for 🚆 for Betten (12km to the northeast). Then 🚠 cable car from Betten valley station to Bettmeralp (runs every 30 minutes from about 6.00 to 23.00, luggage can be checked through to Bettmeralp). From Bettmeralp take the 🚠 gondola to Bettmergrat station on the ridge.

Shorter walks:

1 From Eggishorn by cable car (5h15min, ascent 650m, descent 700m, access as main walk). Follow the main walk to **Eggishorn**, but then descend by cable car to **Fischeralp Kühboden**. Pick up the main walk again at the 5h-point, to return to **Bettmeralp**.

2 Tunnel near Vordersee (4h, ascent 90m, descent 780m, easy, mostly downhill, access as main walk. Follow the main walk, but from the 1h35min-

Making for the Märjelen Hut: a high moor landscape with picturesque lakes

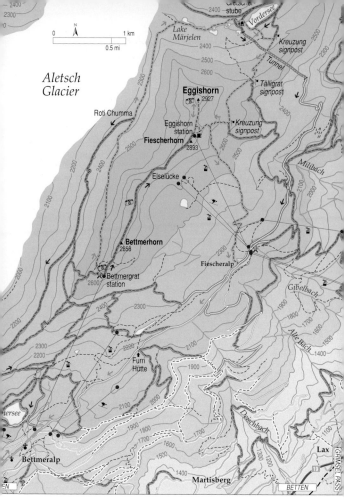

point (**Vordersee**), go through the 1km-long illuminated tunnel which was pierced into the mountain when the dam was built and which now serves walkers. After the tunnel exit, follow signposting to *FIESCHERALP*. From **Fiescheralp** (2h50min) pick up the main walk again at the 5h-point and follow it to the end.

3 Roti Chumma and the Aletsch Glacier (2h45min, ascent under 100m, descent 750m, easy, mostly downhill, access as main walk). Follow the main walk down to the

Roti Chumma junction (45min), then turn sharply back to the left. The trail (signposted throughout to *BETTMERALP*) descends 70m in height before rising again. At a junction 45min past Roti Chumma, keep right and descend gently for 30min, until the trail rises a few metres and reaches a junction. Bear left here, and go straight on at the next junction (just a few metres further on). Then keep left, curving round the mountain ridge. Descend past **Bettmersee** (lake) to **Bettmeralp**.

Alternative walk: High-level ridge trail from Bettmerhorn to Eggishorn (5h30min without Eggishorn cable car, ascent about 400m, descent about 1150m, access as main walk). This highly recommended walk offers a fantastic spectacle, but you must be sure-footed and have a head for heights. *Do not leave the waymarked trail — this is an Alpine hike (waymarked blue-white-blue), for experienced hikers only.* From the Bettmergrat cable car station follow signposting to BETTMERHORN. The path zigzags to the top of **Bettmerhorn** (30min), from where you follow excellent waymarking (every few metres) across ridge-top rocks for about 1.5km. To the north you have an incredible view of the Aletsch Glacier and the Jungfrau/Aletsch/Bietschhorn UNESCO World Natural Heritage Site, and to the south the Rhône and Binn valleys and the mountains of the Valaisian Alps. The trail then drops steeply (there are fixed ropes) to **Elselücke**. From here it's 45 minutes on a wide trail to **Eggishorn** MOUNTAIN STATION with its ski runs (this part is, needless to say, less exhilarating). The ascent from upper Bettmerhorn station to upper Eggishorn station is about 400m, the descent less than 200m, and it takes about 2h30min. From Eggishorn mountain station pick up the main walk at the 3h30min-point, to return to **Bettmeralp** (or descend via Lake Märjelen).

The Aletsch Glacier is the largest glacier in the Alps. It covers about 120km², is more than 20km long and has an ice cover more than 900m deep. The Jungfrau/Aletsch/Bietschhorn UNESCO World

Natural Heritage Site is (to quote UNESCO) 'the most glaciated part of the Alps, containing Europe's largest glacier and a range of classic glacial features such as U-shaped valleys, *cirques,* horn peaks and moraines'.

Walk through the village of **Bettmeralp** to reach the Bettmeralp–Bettmerhorn base station (1982m), and take the gondola up to **Bettmergrat STATION** on the Bettmeralp ridge (2647m). Walking from this upper station, in just a couple of paces you are dazzled by the light reflecting off the icy mass of the awesome Aletsch Glacier.

Follow the signposting for ROTI CHUMMA, gently descending a well-laid path. You reach a junction (**Roti Chumma**, 2369m, **45min**) and continue northwards. The path curves round the north-west ridge of Eggishorn and down to **Lake Märjelen** (2300m, **1h15min**). Then, heading eastwards, the path

starts climbing gently through a high moor landscape with picturesque lakes. Beyond the entrance to a TUNNEL you come to the **Märjelen Hut** (also called 'Gletscherstube') at the **Vordersee** (reservoir, 2360m, **1h35min**). *(Shorter walk 2 turns back here, to the tunnel.)* You could circle the lake clockwise before climbing the Tälligrat (ridge), but the main walk takes a short-cut across the dam wall and follows the trail up the hill (SIGNPOST: **Kreuzung** 2470m, **2h**).

At an intersection (SIGNPOST: **Tälligrat**, 2610m, **2h30min**), the path continues straight on — fairly level for a while, but then rising fairly steeply beyond a junction with another **Kreuzung** SIGNPOST (2623m, **2h45min**), until you reach the **Eggishorn** MOUNTAIN STATION (2869m, **3h30min**). The final path to the top of **Eggishorn** (2927m, **3h50min**) is no problem, and from here you see the entire Aletsch Glacier spread before you.

Return to the mountain station (**4h05min**) and retrace your steps from there for about 15 minutes, then fork sharp right *(no sign, no waymarks)* and follow a narrow mountain path to **Fiescheralp** (also called Kühboden, 2212m, **5h**), the valley station of the Eggishorn cable car. A broad gravel road takes you back via the **Furri Hut** (2172m, **5h35min**) to **Bettmeralp** (**6h10min**).

A well-laid path beside the glacier leads from the Bettmerhorn mountain station to Roti Chumma.

● Index

This index contains only geographical names; for all other entries, see Contents, page 3. Both to save space and to avoid confusion caused by French/German spellings, entries have been grouped by category (eg lakes; rivers). Page numbers in **bold type** indicate photographs; numbers in *italic type* indicate maps; these may be in addition to a text reference on the same page.